ZHE: *[noun] undefined*

Chuck Mike, Antonia Kemi Coker
and Tonderai Munyevu

ZHE: *[noun] undefined*

OBERON BOOKS
LONDON

WWW.OBERONBOOKS.COM

First published in 2013 by Oberon Books Ltd
521 Caledonian Road, London N7 9RH
Tel: +44 (0) 20 7607 3637 / Fax: +44 (0) 20 7607 3629
e-mail: info@oberonbooks.com
www.oberonbooks.com

A catalogue record for this book is available from the British
Library.

PB ISBN: 978-1-78319-072-0
E ISBN: 978-1-78319-571-8

Cover: design by Design237.com
          photography by Tunde Euba

For David Kato, Fanny Ann Eddy, Eric Lemembe, Eudy Simelane and others who have lost their lives in the struggle for equality. And for the many voices around the world who continue to fight against draconian laws simply to be who they are. Also for the many generations to come in the hopes that telling one's story can be a catalyst for liberation and change; acceptance for who you are.

ACKNOWLEDGEMENTS

creators of ZHE: *[noun] undefined* would like to thank the owing individuals and institutions for their assistance and contributions towards bringing the play and its service components into being:

UK: Tunde Euba, Mojisola Adebayo, Stella Barnes, Sandra Cole, Jatinder Verma, Nina Steiger, James Gibbs, Sophie Hook, Catherine McNamara, Anthony Ofoegbu, Ivan Roman Orgaz, Isobel Sullivan, Chika Unaka, Olusola Oyeleye, Julia Reid, Colin Prescod, Jesse Quinones, Dawn Reid, Oladipo Agboluaje, Jelony Osa, Ahmmad Makaddar, Catriona Silver, Steve Marmion, Lizette Nolte, Liz Littlewood, Victoria Shaskan, Frances Ashman, Lisa Goldman, Hackney Empire, Oval House Theatre, Soho Theatre, Gendered Intelligence, Terrence Higgins Trust, The Foyle Foundation, The London Borough of Southwark, Arts Council England, and the LGBTQ community of London.

US: Debbie Mullin, Reed West, Myra Daleng, Deborah Sommers, Dorothy Holland, Johann Stegmeir, Carol Piersol, Cheyenne Varner, dl Hopkins, kb saine, Ted Lewis, Shannon Hooker, John Gunter, Phil Crosby, Don Hooper, Thelma Mike, Archana Pathak, Gwendolyn Dixon, Adrian Rieder, Charles Mike III, Ayanna McMullen, University of Richmond and its Department of Theatre and Dance, The Modlin Center for the Arts, Firehouse Theatre, Centenary College of Louisiana and it's Department of Theatre, The African American Repertory Theatre, Sycamore Rouge, the Save the Firehouse Theatre Project and the LGBTQ community of Richmond.

Zimbabwe: R.B. Ganzva, Diana Malosi, Tawanda Mudonga, B. D. Munyebvu, Gavin Peters, Michael Smith, Ian White, and the LGTBQ community of Harare.

Special thanks to Collective Artistes for making both the production and publication of ZHE: *[noun] undefined* possible.

7

The Collective Artistes production of *ZHE: [noun] undefined* premiered in the UK on 10 October, 2013 at the Burton Taylor Studio, Oxford Playhouse, Oxford, UK. It was directed by Chuck Mike; the music was composed by Juwon Ogungbe with selections from the traditional Zimbabwean and Nigerian domains; designs were by Kate Unwin; the lighting design was by Cis Boyle; the sound design was by Rebecca Smith; the projection designs were by Reed West; the choreography was by Andile Sotiya; the fight choreography was by Robin Colyer; the percussionists were Wale Ogungbe and Clement Ule; the stage manager was Natalie Davies; Sola Oyeleye was the producer. The cast was as follows:

MAN...Tonderai Munyevu

WOMAN ....Antonia Kemi Coker

CHARACTERS

MAN, 30 years old, a Zimbabwean raised in London from age 13.

WOMAN, 48 years old (but looks much younger),
a Nigerian raised in London from birth.

PLACE
Anywhere people listen to stories.

TIME
Today.

'I've Gotta Be Me'

(By Walter Marks and performed by Sammy Davis Jr.)

Whether I'm right or whether I'm wrong
Whether I find a place in this world or never belong
I gotta be me, I've gotta be me
What else can I be but what <u>I am</u>

I want to live, not merely survive
And I won't give up this dream
Of life that keeps me alive
I gotta be me, I gotta be me
The dream that I see makes me what I am

That far-away prize, a world of success
Is waiting for me if I heed the call
I won't settle down, won't settle for less
As long as there's a <u>chance</u> that I can have it all

I'll go it alone, that's how it must be
I can't be right for somebody else
If I'm not right for me
I gotta be free, I've gotta be free
Daring to try, to do it or die
I've gotta be me

I'll go it alone, that's how it must be
I can't be right for somebody else
If I'm not right for me
I gotta be free, I just gotta be free
Daring to try, to do it or die
I gotta be me

9

INTRODUCTION

The first glimpses of *ZHE: [noun] undefined* began in a series of interviews with Tonderai and Antonia on 29 July, 2009 at the Oval House Theatre, London. I had known Antonia for well over a decade. We worked together on several shows and grew to be close friends. Tonderai and I had only met personally once and yet he was about to unfold very intimate details of his life.

I had been after Antonia for many years to tell her story in a one-woman show and she had been reticent. We had just completed a production of *The African Company Presents Richard III* by Carlye Brown in which she played a progressive black actress based in New York City before Lincoln freed the slaves. Antonia felt empowered by this experience and was finally inspired to attempt her life narrative on stage. Within this period she had met Tonderai and in her interactions with him mistook him for a female. This was an act that touched her deeply and painfully as she had frequently been falsely identified as a man. The two became fuelled by the notion to do something theatrical about mistaken gender identity. I felt that simply telling the world about their lives from the onset would speak to this need and several other concerns that I'd sensed buried deep within their spirits.

Both had lived challenging lives as gay Africans growing up in the UK. Antonia had mentioned some of the difficult times in her upbringing but had detailed nothing as heart-rending as I was about to hear. I encouraged them to start with recollections from childhood that they were comfortable with. If and when they chose difficult paths I remained supportive, listening with an open heart and a caring mind. This pattern of information gathering, reflection, and analysis (though infinitely less formalized) would be shared between us for the next few years. Over three continents, innumerable good meals and several bottles of suitable wine our friendships would deepen as our lives intertwined. Like the process, our creation would be devised. Though documentary in substance there would be improvisation, poetic scripting, dance, music and physical theatre.

Antonia had been visibly disturbed by moments within the interview session but left comforted and with some sense of relief that the journey had begun. Tonderai had an upcoming therapist appointment and upon departing noted that he felt as if he had already had the session. (This moment began the inside joke about me being 'the therapist' in the play.)

As I departed the theatre alone, that day took on a surreal ambience. The cassette tapes I carried far outweighed the plastic which encased them. The enormity of the exercise became viscerally translucent to me. With several decades of theatre experience working on social issues I'd never felt such depth in terms of personal responsibility. These were living characters whose lives were 'in process' and my connection to them was deeply personal. Our drama would be life impacting not just for them but for anyone who came across it.

It became clear to me that our skills as theatre-makers alone would be insufficient for this task. Healing would be part of the journey and it would take a reservoir of love and endless courage on their part to tell these stories truthfully. A credible celebration of their lives would also strengthen them for further pursuit of the single solitary quest to simply be 'me'.

The lyrics to Sammy Davis Jr's 'I've Gotta Be Me' speak profoundly to the experiences of people who walk the unbeaten path of difference, particularly for those living between and outside accepted identities – whether this be their genders, sexualities or cultures.

Creating ZHE has been a long excursion for Antonia, Tonderai and myself. The four-year voyage of development has been sometimes painful, other times joyous but often fearful. Walking into the unknown of one's personal life journey can be as daunting and terrifying as it is empowering. For us, 'truth' has been at the heart of this adventure. Telling the truth of these passages, experiencing and processing the truth through our development and rehearsal process and living the truth on stage. It is with this commitment to authenticity, and we have questioned the meaning of that word numerous times, that we have dared to peel back the layers of two people's journeys to reveal the evolution of lives that have been both tormented and shaped by their existence outside easy definitions.

Most of us are born the way we are. Few question these identities; and fewer brave the challenges of speaking out about their experience in multiplicity outside the binaries that society likes to assign to identity. Lesbian... Gay... Bi-sexual... Transgender... Queer... Questioning... Intersex... Antonia and Tonderai may have been perceived in these terms at various points in their lives, but what they both want is simply to be who they are without societal labels. (I've Gotta Be Me!)

We are aware that the textbook definition of zhe suggests those who have made a decision to identify themselves in a genderless space – neither male nor female. 'Zhe' implies a space of non-specificity and a 'blur' of the known. For us the word has come to signify a blurring of many identity markers. We assume that anyone who chooses to occupy the space delineated by 'zhe'

simply wants to be themselves ('me').
So our play is really about the fluidity of gender and identity. In sharing these stories our hope is that anyone sitting before us will join us in celebrating life in all its complexity with a view towards engendering the tolerance needed to create a better world.

Chuck Mike
27 September, 2013

The Script in Chapters

This is a true story

Staging Note

Breathing is perhaps the simplest cadence of life. How it manifests in this play is fundamental to capturing the earnest collective journey of these characters and the audiences. For those who choose to re-enact this script, your portrayals will undoubtedly be marked by breathing of your own, in doing so we ask that you also consider well those breaths that are signposted here. The truth of these characters may well be found in making the journey itself.
Breathe.

PROLOGUE

A visual appears.

For nearly two decades theatre-maker Chuck Mike had been trying to get Antonia Kemi Coker to tell her personal story theatrically.

In 2009 there was a catalyst. Antonia met Tonderai Munyevu.

These are their stories as told to Chuck Mike.

WOMAN
    It was a mistake.
    Not the random kind that is easily overlooked.
    Well at least not by me.
    It was a chance encounter at an audition.
    I was a cast member helping to audition people.
    She was cute.

MAN
    Like a rose near full bloom
    Or a peacock crossing the road.
    But without the beard
    And with far more weight.

WOMAN
    We chatted about the play,

MAN & WOMAN
    That brave African Theatre Company,
    Who dared, before slaves were set free
    To act a play of Shakespeare
    And jailed they were,
    Only to rebel once more by telling
    Stories about themselves instead.

WOMAN
    Her smile was beguiling.
    There was an attractive reservation about her.
    She told me about her day job,
    Waiting tables,
    And a play that she was in at the moment.

MAN
>Two Gents.

WOMAN
>She went her way
>And I mine.
>That night intrigued
>I thought,

MAN & WOMAN
>*(MAN sarcastically.)* She was different.

WOMAN
>I made enquiries.

MAN
>*(Cynically.)* About the girl,

MAN & WOMAN
>The cute *girl* with the beguiling smile –
>Attractively reserved.

MAN
>*(With infinite clarity.)* 'He's not a she. He's a he.'

ANTONIA
>It was a mistake. Not the random kind that is easily
>overlooked.

MAN & WOMAN
>Well at least not by me.

WOMAN
>I tried to apologize but,

MAN & WOMAN
>It glanced the ear and bypassed the heart.

WOMAN
>And it was *so* important to me
>Because I have had a lifetime,

MAN & WOMAN
>Of people thinking I am who I am not.

WOMAN

It was a *big* mistake
By ME and I *needed* to be forgiven –
To be OK with me.

MAN

It *was* a chance encounter at an audition,
I came to try out.
She looked radiantly rugged.

WOMAN

Definitely the peacock type.

MAN

We did chat about the play.

MAN & WOMAN

Those marvellous African players
who performed Shakespeare
and with their backs against a prison wall
found freedom by
telling stories about themselves instead.

MAN

She looked very strong
And much older than me.

WOMAN

Forty-three.

MAN

And I a mere twenty-six.
She *was* confident.
Knew how to take her space in a room.

WOMAN

(Bluntly.) Manly.

MAN

Mmmm,
But gentle and wise,
And we did talk about my day job.

WOMAN
  Waiter

MAN
  Maître d'

WOMAN
  Oops

MAN
  And the play I was in – *Two Gents* – that should have been
  a clue.

WOMAN
  It did set me thinking.

MAN
  But *I* kind of knew *she* was a she.
  Thinking that *I* was a she.
  And her apology –
  I'd heard the like so many times before.

MAN & WOMAN
  It glanced the ear and bypassed the heart.

MAN
  I guess really being sorry
  Means never having to say it.

WOMAN
  And maybe *real* forgiveness comes from a special place

MAN & WOMAN
  Where people breathe *(They breathe.)* and tell stories about
  themselves.

CHAPTER 1: EARLY CHILDHOOD MEMORIES
OF MUM IN ZIMBABWE

MAN
  Y'know there's a phrase in Zimbabwe, *'pane nyaya'* –
  'there's a story' and that's what my grandmother used to

call me *'pane nyaya'*. My story starts in Harare, Zimbabwe.
My earliest memory was 'getting ready' for mum. My mum
was this glamorous figure, this exciting, vibrant woman
who was very well-to-do and wanted to do the best for her
family

WOMAN

my mum wanted to do the best for her family too but I
don't think she quite pulled it off

MAN

and so that sort of transferred to how she dressed and
looked. The things I remember about her is perfume, red
lipstick – white clothes – she had this fur jacket that she
used to wear to work in the morning

WOMAN

my mum was a really hard worker, liked clothes as well,
yeah she made stuff,

MAN

and I'd stay at home with the maid and throughout the day
the maid –

WOMAN

Maid?

MAN

would be saying 'stop doing that' and 'when your mum
comes I'll tell her' and 'when your mum comes she will
know about this'… We had this lovely dog called Lido

WOMAN

I had a dog called Sheba – it was a mongrel

MAN

and he was cream and very fluffy, very beloved of
the family, and the dog also loved my mum. We all
had this sense in her absence of her return being very
overpowering, very much the centre of the day, the centre
of our existence, all of us. To this day there are some
memories of her that linger on – no doubt – if I hear a

certain sound or I smell a certain thing like Poison, she wears Poison, a Christian Dior perfume, called Poison, even that suggests this sort of danger and attainment of glamour. I think that *Dynasty* was on TV at that time so there was that Diahann Carroll, Alexis Carrington sort of dressing because she could have things made for her. She loved to entertain so the home in itself was a showcase for her, an extension of her character. So even now if I smell Poison, the first thought that comes to my mind is my mother.

WOMAN

I have no memory of smell of my mum…

MAN

The first, is an emotional reaction of delight but slightly mixed with this sense of apprehension: Am I in the right place? Am I dressed the right way? What will she say? That was, that is for me still connected to that smell. Then there's the intense colour red, her lipstick. A couple of Christmases ago we got her four shades of Chanel red lipstick and that really took us back to that time as children when we were growing up – my brother and my sister – we didn't like the maid you know she represented my mother's authority *(The MAID shoves MAN down and commences to bathe him.)* but obviously wasn't my mother herself. She was from the rural areas so she didn't understand anything but could follow the rules, just to

MAID

'get the kids ready'

MAN

so sometimes we'd get punished by the maid for

MAID

'trying to get her fired',

MAN

for

MAID

'trying to ruin her life'

MAN

she'd be very strict with us and the MAIN thing…the absolute main thing was that at about four o'clock we would start getting ready…so forget what you're wearing after school… I'd need to discard that and go find some proper trousers or a shirt and she would bath me. She had this stone she used to rub against me all over, especially my feet just to get this dirt off and as a child I remember just being forced into the bathtub. She'd put this soap in my hair and just rub it over and I remember my eyes stinging from the soap running over and of course she's in a hurry because she's got a thousand other things to do so then I'd start crying and she'd slap me,

MAID

'be quiet', 'get ready'

MAN

a rinse, pat down with a towel and then *Vaseline* – get moisturized to glow. I was finally put in these clothes which would last me from about four-thirty to seven when mum came. *(They pause to listen as Lido barks.)* We would normally hear the dog barking, I guess he could smell Mum coming from afar and he would just rush off and this would be sometime after six. I followed Lido, running to the gate to see my mum and the dog would bark, bark, bark and get very excited. But he never touched my mother because she always used to wear white. And I, would be standing there waiting. She was always very excited to see me but the main thing I remember was, *(MAID picks up bags and moves, they follow mum.)* that sense of rushing towards her but not really having any immediate contact with her, standing there, waiting. AND then she'd just come in.

Two hours later I was in bed *(Cocktail sounds and theme from Dynasty are heard in the background.)* and all of her friends were arriving – I could hear glasses clinking – I tried to put myself to sleep, then sounds of laughter, I just kept hearing glasses clinking – then finally, I would open the door, see them, look at them, what they were doing – and then one person might be going to the bathroom then I would panic and rush back into bed –

WOMAN
but in your dad's house?

MAN
and that's how I'd fall asleep every night in my mum's house

WOMAN
it was a completely different story, wasn't it?

MAN
hearing the sounds of people –

WOMAN
when you got to your dad's house *(Pause.)*

CHAPTER 2: EARLY CHILDHOOD MEMORIES OF DAD AND ZIMBABWE

MAN
Most of my friends called me Choza –

WOMAN
Choza?

MAN
Yes which means a boy that is really a girl.

WOMAN
Really?

MAN
It was affectionate, a name that fit, a celebration of me. *(A group of children do a call and response song to celebrate Choza. He joins in culminating in a brief dance.)*

My brother and sister still call me that.

23

WOMAN
(With final affection.) Choza.

MAN
In my dad's house it was a completely different story, nothing was in its full place.

Dad used to drink a lot

WOMAN
my dad too

MAN
my dad used to drink a lot so sometimes he'd never come back home and when he did he would threaten to 'cancel it' – whatever it was that one wanted to do.

MUDHARA
I will cancel it. Ndozvikanzura. I will cancel everything!

MAN
But this was when Zimbabwe got its independence and a lot of people were feeling the good times that were coming.

WOMAN
Not the same for us, it was cold in England. They were racist.

MAN
My dad had moved from rural Rusape to Harare as an accountant and he was the best dressed man in the world,

WOMAN
my dad was quite a snazzy dresser as well

MAN
my father was the first person I ever saw with those things, I don't know what they're called – they hold your shirt down

WOMAN
arm bracelets, yeah

MAN

> and they used to be gold and elastic and made of some
> kind of silver material – and he used to have those pink
> shirts before anybody wore pink shirts – and contrasting
> ties –

WOMAN

> nothing too flashy then –

MAN

> it was all very understated – very English. Somehow he
> had noticed some white people on the road and how they
> dressed and I think he kind of got his dressing from them –

WOMAN

> so as a rural boy he learned the way

MAN

> and he was also the life and soul of the party

WOMAN

> my dad too

MAN

> that's why I never saw him at home – everybody wanted
> to know

MAN & WOMAN

> where is your father we're having a party on Saturday,
> where is he

MAN

> and because he was never at home, whenever we had to
> stay with him, we had to do things ourselves

WOMAN

> my dad was at home most of the time

MAN

> and when my brother and sister – 'cause they were
> teenagers at this stage – went out, I had to look after myself
> sometimes

WOMAN

me too

MAN

and so when I was eight I'd have to make my own food. I remember one time, *(He demonstrates.)* trying to make porridge and I got it all wrong. This massive bit of hot liquid poured on me – agonizing – and when you wipe off something like that some of your skin actually comes off, and I remember this as if it was yesterday – of feeling the pain but not being able to express it, and then screaming and shouting and running outside to try to get some help, some sympathy from someone. When he did come home, he was drunk – he used to leave his money on the side table – and I remember my brother and I used to sneak in late at night because we knew he was so drunk and so fast asleep – and take some of his money. *(MUDHARA catches him in the act.)*

WOMAN

I took money from my dad too.

MAN

Those were the good times, I think that's where I learned everything about dressing, about looking good – that's one thing my mother always gave him credit for

MAMA MAN

at least he knows how to dress.

MAN

Back at my mother's house I would notice that things were different – her friends were still coming along and I still had to get dressed up, made to look pretty and English, but the space had become smaller and smaller. My bedroom, I started sharing it with my brother – he and I would be in bunk beds and at one point my sister had a sleeping bag in the same room. My mother started bringing lodgers into the house.

WOMAN
My dad had lodgers too.

MAN
I think things just got too much for her. It was the
beginning for many, of the exodus from Zimbabwe to
England – so she decided that she would move to England
to find a better job to support all of us, so we had to live
with my dad full-time. Things changed. My dad was still
the life of the party, the bee's knees…

WOMAN
same as mine

MAN
and not always coming home. So when my sister also left
I realized that something had to change. I headed for Mt.
St Joseph's Missionary Boarding School. That was the
beginning of a whole new life for me. The first intense
memory that I have was of my high school history teacher,
Mr. Hwamwe. I remember being in class and he asked a
question, just a normal question, and I didn't really know
the answer but I thought I knew it sort of at the back of my
mind and I put my hand up.

MR HWAMWE
'Tonderai'

MAN
I think um that it is…

MR HWAMWE
That's good!

MAN
He applauded me not for the answer itself but for having
been brave enough to put my hand up and suggest
something, something I wasn't sure about. That made my
day. I think it was the nicest thing that anyone has ever
said to me, to be commended for the bravery of actually
offering something. He was very good-looking…tall…
black…gorgeous, straight man – devastating. I think it

was the beginning of me feeling very uh, very – starting to know that I had a way with men that wasn't just masculine – pane nyaya – it wasn't sexual at the time, it was just that he was – so impressive to me – like no one else I've ever seen. He was great. Just a very different person.

CHAPTER 3: EARLY CHILDHOOD MEMORIES OF MUM & DAD IN EAST LONDON

WOMAN

I was also a post-independence baby. Nigeria cut the British loose in 1960 and within the decade my parents had come over to England. They left my older sister, Tola behind. I was born here. I think my earliest memories would be when I was about four. I'm living in a place called Plaistow in East London. I grew up mostly with a nanny because my parents were either at work or studying

MAN

Nanny, hmmm did she by any chance bath you?

WOMAN

and within that environment– late 60s, early 70s – Plaistow was an all-white working-class neighbourhood – black kids weren't treated very well. People would call you names;

WHITE NEIGHBOURS

'wog', 'black bastard', 'go back to your own country'.

WOMAN

Kind of confusing to me 'cause – it *was* my country! I remember going to the sweetshop down the road. The woman named Vera who owned it would say

VERA *(In Cockney.)*

It must be cold for you in terms of where you come from.

WOMAN

I'm thinking 'I just come from up the road.' Our house was close to West Ham football stadium, after a game whether they won or lost you shouldn't be there. *(Threatening*

sounds of crowd roars.) They were looking for a fight with
the visiting team but any blacks who happened to be on
the street would do. Funny 'cause when I think back now,
they were one of the first to hire a black footballer, Clyde
Best. Our house had a garden full of weeds, overgrown
and unkempt. I used to bury my dollies there when they
broke. My dad owned the house and we had lodgers.
('Mukulumuke' plays faintly in the background.) We used to go
to parties all the time, visiting other Nigerians, birthdays,
weddings and christenings. Us kids had a great time
running in and out of rooms, dancing, laughing, eating chin
chin and drinking Pepsi. *(The children sing 'Mukulumuke' with
a brief dance. MAN & WOMAN take a breath together concluding
the child's play.)* Apart from his studies, my dad worked in
a car lot. He was exceptionally charming, good dresser,
funny, proud, made people laugh. Very bright. He was a
Cheribim and Seraphin church member. You know – those
people that wear all white. My sister would later tell me
that

TOLA

he was a churchgoer – not a Christian

WOMAN

He loved to drink, Long Life lager and smoked Consulate
cigarettes. I can still remember the smell of the menthol.
And he could sing. He called himself

PAPA WOMAN

the maaaan with the golden voice… *(He sings a brief song,
'Irin Ajo'.WOMAN joins in.)*

WOMAN

He was funny. I really really loved him. And I must have
been a mischief maker because the words I remember
hearing from him most often was

PAPA WOMAN
Kemi take advice.

WOMAN

And I never really did.

MAN

And what about your mother?

WOMAN

(Disinterested.) A devout Catholic. Named me after a black saint.

MAN

And…

WOMAN *(More reluctantly.)*

She was studying too…worked in a factory

MAN

Yes…

WOMAN

Ok so she brought me mints! She worked at the Trebor mint factory. The fact is that I really loved my dad. Didn't like what he did to my mum, but I loved him…and her too I suppose. The relationship between them was very violent. *(We hear faint sounds of struggle and shouting.)* Some of the time Mum was in the hospital. There was one time my dad beat her up so bad that she ran out of the house but then came back to bath me and I remember begging her, begging her

WOMAN CHILD

(Fearful.) leave, please mummy, please LEAVE… *(The sound of a small child's voice repeating this lingers in the air.)*

WOMAN

Mum left for Nigeria when I was four and the story that I've been told is that I was supposed to go with her, but my dad didn't want me to go so he pretended he had a ticket for me. *(Airport sounds.)* I remember being in my best dress. Anyway, the ticket was never bought – so my mum went off and he told her

DAD

Ah, ah – you don't worry, I will send her tomorrow.

WOMAN

The next day and the next day came and he never sent me – and I was missing my mum. He had girlfriends but I never felt any of them could take her place. I wanted to go to Nigeria to see her and the sister I had never met. Nigeria held some mystery to me. Now it held my mum. It was a bit difficult being brought up by a man and that was odd in the 70s; a man bringing up a girl. My dad bought me – a yellow nylon night dress – and he sent me to school in it. I tried to explain to him it was a *night dress* –

DAD

Kemi – night, day, it's a dress – take advice.

WOMAN

So I had to go to school in it. The kids laughed and I was teased the whole day. *(Beat.)* Dad used to keep money under a lamp – just spare change, so when he'd go out I'd get the money and go and buy sweets for people just to make friends. I got caught *(PAPA WOMAN smacks her hand.)* and that was trouble. My dad used to lock me in the house when he went to work but I had my TV and food so it was kind of okay. I remember smoking tea bags in his pipe and

MAN & WOMAN

making concoctions

WOMAN

I wouldn't have been more than seven or eight. Sometimes I'd climb out the window, and play out with my mates. I'd have one person at the top of the street to check if my dad's coming and they'd be like

FRIEND

'Camay'

WOMAN

My Nigerian name is Kemi but they pronounced it Camay.

FRIEND

'Camay' – your dad's coming

ANTONIA

I replaced it with my Catholic name – Antonia. One time my dad caught me, just as I jumped back through the window into the front room. I got a beating that day. At the age of eight a woman I now call Auntie Jane worked as a dinner lady at my school. *(Sound of rain.)* When it rained we would all run to the tin roofed shelter and she would hold my hand. One day she said

AUNTY JANE

'ask your dad if you can come and visit me on Saturday afternoons'.

ANTONIA

Because she didn't live far away Dad said yes. *(Beat.)* I told lies in school. I just tried to make things as regular as the white peoples' lives were, you know like, saying I was going on holiday to Spain and I wasn't going anywhere – or that we were eating sausage and mash with salad for dinner and we were eating eba with egusi soup. Well, all the lies I had told about having English food became true 'cause those were the things I ate at Auntie Jane's. She would buy me sweets and clothes. She would take me to see her blind mother in hospital. I remember kissing Nanny Rose hello and thinking she's never gonna know I'm black 'cause we never ever mentioned my colour. Auntie Jane would take me to church on Sunday and if we were late she would say

AUNTIE JANE

'Tone put your best foot forward'.

ANTONIA

People often asked her if she had adopted me and she would say

AUNTIE JANE

'No she's just a little girl I know'.

32

WOMAN

Sometimes I would ask for big presents like a bike. She would carefully explain to me

AUNTY JANE

'Oh Toni, you know I love you very much. But I'm not actually your mum and big things like bikes are what parents get for their children.'

WOMAN

Auntie Jane was a saviour. Even when horrible things happened, I always had Saturday to look forward to or a holiday that she'd be taking me on. One day I asked her 'why are you so good to me *(AUNTY JANE points up to the sky.)* and we never said any more about it. *(Beat.)* I wasn't being particularly good in school. One time during swimming lessons, the water was cold, so none of us kids wanted to get in *(A few kids sit at the pool side with their teacher watching on.)*

KID 1

(Teeth chattering.) It's cold!

KID 2

Brrrrr... It's cold!!

WOMAN

It's cold!!!!

TEACHER

Antonia of course it's not cold. *(She pushes ANTONIA into the pool.)*

WOMAN

I splattered and struggled and barely made it to the poolside and when I got out... *(She slaps the TEACHER around her waist and runs off.)*

PAPA WOMAN

This letter says you hit a teacher.

WOMAN

In Nigeria people believe you are lucky to be educated in England.

PAPA WOMAN

Ohhhhh, you this girl. Your sister Tola is even putting herself through school and here you are in England messing about. I SAY IS IT TRUE YOU HIT A TEACHER!

WOMAN

Yes but… *(He kicks her.)*

MAN

GET OUT! You useless girl.

WOMAN

… I never really got over that. That's when I stopped caring about formal education.

CHAPTER 4: SHIFTING BETWEEN MUM & DAD – RUNNING AWAY

The sounds of small children playing. A musical fantasia is also heard as they play tag.

With all my antics that I got up to being left home alone, Dad decided to put me with a child minder to keep me safe. The family was from Antigua. They had two boys and a girl. I loved running up and down the house with her kids. I wanted to play with my big sister but she lived in Nigeria so I really loved the games we played. *(They accidentally encounter each other and scream.)*

CHILD

Hide and Seek! *(The children play hide and seek. After a brief search WOMAN finds a place to hide…)*

WOMAN

The mother was a real nice woman.

CHILD

One

WOMAN
She would go to work and leave us with her husband.

CHILD
Two

WOMAN
I really can't remember much about him, only that he was quiet.

CHILD
Three

WOMAN
There were times when this man would watch us play

CHILD
Four

WOMAN
then he would call me into a room.

MAN & WOMAN
We would all stop running

CHILD
Five

WOMAN
I would walk slowly to him

CHILD
Six

MAN
as the boys looked on. He closed the door,

CHILD
Seven

WOMAN
And held me gently by the shoulders

CHILD
Eight

MAN & WOMAN
and pushed me down on the couch.

CHILD
Nine

MAN
His face

WOMAN
was rough

MAN
and prickly,

CHILD
Ten

WOMAN
I tasted cigarettes.

MAN
Eleven

WOMAN
I wanted my dad to come and take me home but I couldn't tell him. He would have killed him

CHILD
Twelve

WOMAN
and gone to jail, then there would be no one to look after me.

CHILD
Thirteen

WOMAN
I think the mother knew but she didn't say anything. I knew it was wrong

CHILD
Fourteen

WOMAN

and I couldn't tell anyone. It didn't happen every day but I knew it could happen at any time.

CHILD

COMING READY OR NOT! *(What follows is a breath moment denied.)*

WOMAN

When I was ten my dad travelled to Nigeria without me –

MAN

You OK?

WOMAN

I'm fine. When I was ten my... *(To MAN.)* Are you OK?

MAN

Yea, I'm fine, I'm fine.

WOMAN

You sure. *(Beat. They continue.)* When I was ten.

WOMAN

When I was ten Dad travelled to Nigeria without me. He left me with a friend of my mum who had six children so I was always on the bottom. We had second-hand clothes and sometimes we couldn't go on school trips. When Dad and Mum came back my mum won custody of me but that didn't work out. *(Dad paces disgruntled in the background.)* She wanted me to knit and sew and stuff like that. She didn't want me to play football, she wanted me to just stay home and cook and clean and sweep, whereas with my dad

PAPA WOMAN AND WOMAN

We sweep when we want to sweep, we eat when we want to eat, we watch football together. O ti to.[1]

WOMAN

I was used to playing out on the street. I pissed standing up 'cause that's what I saw my dad do.

---

[1] Yoruba expression for 'that is enough'.

PAPA WOMAN
That's my girl…

WOMAN
and I didn't wash my hands after I used the toilet and all this made her furious. She got quite violent towards me. That's when I began running away. My dad gained custody of me again but our relationship was never the same. It wasn't working with him either. Whenever I made mention of my mum, he started cursing and yelling

PAPA WOMAN
'that woman'

WOMAN
this and

PAPA WOMAN
'that woman'

WOMAN
that. He never said 'your mum' he always called her

PAPA WOMAN
'that woman'.

WOMAN
I think he must have thought she was rubbing off on me. I began to run away from him too. I even slept in a car for a while.

CHAPTER 5: CARE STORIES

Sounds of children playing over music and vocals. A physical celebration of the narrative which follows takes place. A game of pool is on.

Although it didn't feel like normal life I really liked being in the kids' home. They gave me a lot of pocket money, lots of food, and they were not allowed to hit me. There were thirteen kids between the ages of eleven and eighteen and seven of us were black. We enjoyed listening to soul music, cracking jokes and taking every opportunity to wind each other and the staff up. We played rounders in the garden, pool in the kitchen and argued over every shot and ball hit.

KID 1

It was LOUD – shouting – was normal talk.

WOMAN

Nobody wanted to be – out.

KID 2

Yea. Nobody wanted to be 'out'.

WOMAN

And if you were losing at pool – *(She cheats by disrupting his shot. They rile each other up.)*

KID 3

I saw that

WOMAN

What, what, what, what…

KID THREE

I saw that, I saw that…. *(KID THREE kisses his teeth as they sit down in the bus.)*

WOMAN

They took us on holiday once a year to Great Yarmouth or Southend. We would go in a big yellow bus with

MAN&WOMAN

Newham Local Authority

WOMAN

written on the side.

MAN & WOMAN

SHAME!

WOMAN

We all ducked our heads until the bus pulled out of London. There were two black women amongst the staff and I'm still in touch with them. Before then staff were changing all the time. I never told many people in school that I was in care 'cause most people think kids in care are bad. All the kids in my home were there 'cause their families had broken down. If you did do something wrong it got reported in an 'incident book' and you could lose privileges. I tried to be good so I wouldn't miss youth theatre after school.

KID 4

Psst…psst… *(Pretends to be a paparazzo; he takes a shot.)* *(Teasing.)* She wants to be a movie star.

KID 5

Yea, go to Hollywood. *(He giggles on his way.)*

WOMAN

I loved the cleaners, they were always singing. I had learned a lot of songs in a school play from the Second World War. We would all sing them together. *(A cleaner and WOMAN sing a few times miming and dancing: 'We're going to hang out the washing on the Siegfried Line, have you any dirty washing mother dear.')*

CLEANER

Ooo Tone you know that one too ey. You were born in the wrong year.

WOMAN

There were three pretty popular black girls there and I was one of them. We called ourselves

MAN & WOMAN

The Sambo Sisters! *(They gush a very brief improvised melody… Da, da, da, da, Da Whooooo.)*

WOMAN

We used to sneak out to parties. After lights out we'd get dressed up, stuff our bed with pillows and clothes *(They climb out the window and down the fire escape checking to make sure no one sees them.)* and off to the local club to dance to soul music and party with the big men dem. *(At the disco*

brief antics of excitement precede McFadden and Whitehead's
'Ain't No Stoppin Us Now' which sends them into a dance frenzy.)
On the way back we'd be freezing waiting for the night
bus. One day we came back and knew we'd gotten busted
'cause our bed was scattered with clothing...

Then there was Uncle Jim – loved him. He was a care
worker. Called me

UNCLE JIM
foghorn mouth

WOMAN
'cause I was loud.

UNCLE JIM
Antonia you are just a stroppy adolescent.

WOMAN
He was a skinny white man who used to wear flares but
he didn't care. Very strict. If you were two minutes late
he'd make life miserable for you. He'd come to the club
and embarrass you. You'd be there getting down with the
moves and this white man comes in, takes the microphone
and calls out everybody's name.

UNCLE JIM
Victoria Shaskan, Tamara Malcolm, Antonia Coker,
surprise surprise, from Thirty-Seven Marsdon Road.
CHILDREN'S HOME. You were supposed to be back by
nine. It is now nine-0-five!

UNCLE JIM & WOMAN
SHAME.

WOMAN
I remember fretting one time 'cause I had a history exam
but I hadn't revised. When I told him he said;

UNCLE JIM
'You're an actor. Make it up.'

WOMAN

And I passed. *(Beat.)* There was this place called the 'quiet room'. *(She listens to music in the quiet room, it is a piano version of Burt Bacharach's 'A House is not a Home'.)* I loved it. You could to go in there and be all by yourself and listen to music. The opportunity to be alone and just sit was a real privilege but you had to earn it. I actually got to go in there quite a few times.

MAN

Really.

WOMAN

Well maybe a couple of times. *(MAN interjects again.)* OK once. I used to visit Dad at weekends but never heard much from my mum. One evening after ten a social worker came to my room.

SOCIAL WORKER

Antonia. How are you getting along. You know if I'm here this late it's for a big reason. *(WOMAN shrugs her shoulders.)*

SOCIAL WORKER

Your mum's dead.

WOMAN

I think I said 'I don't care.' And asked to go to bed. I didn't go to the funeral.

MAN

(A breath moment.) That's sad.

WOMAN

I didn't know how to handle it. *(Continuing the story.)* When next I saw my dad I told him casually whilst we were walking on the street – 'that woman' died. He broke into tears. I was so surprised. I thought he didn't like her.

CHAPTER 6: BOARDING SCHOOL

The boarding school was on a mountain, West of Harare.
I ended up in the worst dormitory you could find. Some
people had a space with four, eight, twelve people; I ended
up with eighteen people in my dormitory.

WOMAN
I know what that's like

MAN
and I was a bed-wetter

WOMAN
me too.

MAN
It was a Catholic Missionary School; so, slowly, I became
very religious, and yet…sensually awakened all at the
same time. For my school uniform I wore a blue shirt,
striped blue and white tie, grey shorts, long grey stockings
and black shoes. In the winter we would add long grey
trousers, blue woolen sweaters and for me, a very long,
custom-made scarf, naturally I added a layer of thick soles
to my black shoes to give me a little extra height – actually
an extra strut. Everyone loved me. They'd talk about
'ngochani',[2] I didn't know what that meant. I had never
heard *it* mentioned – I never considered *it* – I remember
my grandmother when I was growing up saying

GRANDMA
Pane nyaya, you're not going to be doing any of *that*

MAN
but she never told me what 'that' was– and clearly she
knew what I was. In school there was a disco every
Saturday…hormones raging, the generator overworked
would shut down and the lights would go off. The rules
said you needed to go to your dormitories and sleep… I
remember getting to my dormitory, I actually took it all

---

[2] Shona expression for homosexual

seriously – 'oh the lights have gone off, I guess we have to go to bed'… So I got into my bed and slept. And then, like five minutes later, I sort of felt this movement at the bottom of my bed. Sort of like a hand coming through. And then like a person, and I thought 'Oh that's strange there is a person in my bed'. And then I recall smelling this person. I've never been that close to someone physically to smell them. I remember thinking that's a different scent, that's how people smell when they are close to you. But I actually didn't know who this person was. I had no idea. And he just sort of, at first he lay down next to me and then I just sort of tried to respond. But I didn't know exactly what was going on. I remember there was no kissing. I just remember my body being moved and I didn't know what to do back so I just sort of allowed myself to move with whatever was happening. Then two minutes later – wetness – and that was it. And then he left just as inconspicuously as he'd come. It was like a memory, a distant – but real memory. Subsequently, I thought who was this person? And why me? What signal did I send off. And then I got used to it. I got used to it. On occasions I crept into other peoples' beds too, sometimes with my heart in my mouth 'cause you don't want to creep into some macho man's bed.

WOMAN

How did you know?

MAN

I don't know *how* I knew. But I always knew. When this hand, as soon as I crept in, this amiable hand would just help me along – I quickly knew I was in the right place. And then, I remember, I used to read letters from my mum out loud so people could tell that they were from England. *(Classmates stand behind him peering over his shoulder and making comments to each other on the content.)*

WOMAN *(Reading the letter as MAMA MAN.) Dear Tonde, I hope you are doing well and reading hard. Thank you for the pictures you sent. You look so smart in your uniform. You seem a bit taller.*

Either you have grown a bit or you have added soles to your shoes.
I hope you liked the scarf I sent you, you must take care of it. I got
it from Harrods, one of the most exclusive shops here so don't lose
it! London is frightfully cold so we thank God for the underground
that gives some respite when going to work. If only it would not be
so packed. There is nothing like being so close to someone that you
can physically smell them. Imagine. (The children laugh and MAN,
miffed, takes letter and continues reading.)

MAN *(as his mother.)*
    Nevertheless, we thank God for his mercies. I am prospering and
    the beautiful snowfall has covered everywhere providing light
    in this place where there is often none. I hope the money I sent
    you through your dad was enough. I am sure you would have
    quickly gone and bought roast chicken and sadza[3] for you and
    your mates from that woman you have raved about so much. I am
    working hard to bring you and your brother here for Christmas
    so we will all be together again. Write soon and be well darling.
    Love, Mummy. PS: Remember to use your scrubbing stone well,
    particularly on the feet and don't forget to moisturize. You are
    in the mountains and it gets dry so keep warm. (The sound of
    drums occur faintly. Du du du du dun du du du du dun. It is a
    common rhythm associated with Shona Catholicism. The song
    'Garai Nesu' filters in.) There was this priest, Father Makoni,
    who was a bit reckless. There was a rumour around of
    him being a bit of a boozer. He used to have this Land
    Rover and would drive by and leave dust in his wake in
    the afternoon. There were always *stories* about him. When
    he led mass it was quite interesting. This priest you'd seen
    during the day *(FATHER MAKONI enters.)* just being a normal
    person would enter through this shaft of light suddenly in
    these cream majestic long robes. After a fourth former had
    done his reading of the day, it was time for Father Makoni
    to deliver his daily homily. He would always start by
    clearing his throat,

FATHER MAKONI
    UmgrUmumumumummmmm

---

[3] Zimbabwean cooked corn meal

MAN

a sound which for some reason in our minds resonated with the generator from last night's disco – and he would start,

FATHER MAKONI

I keep seeing things.

MAN

And we'd all just put our heads down; 'I hope it wasn't me.' And there was this wondering about 'who did he see' from the podium.

FATHER MAKONI

(Clears throat again.) I keep seeing things.

MAN

And we'd all go, *(Terrified.)* 'I hope it wasn't me… I hope it wasn't me…' With all of the sex that was going on if you were caught trying to get to the other dormitory in the middle of the night it was often by this priest because he kept late hours.

FATHER MAKONI

I hope you know every action has consequences and some of these consequences you don't want to know.

MAN

Our hearts were within a moment of stopping because there was a threat of him saying it's *you* that he saw last night. So then we're all waiting for him to finish but then he'd go off on a tangent. *(FATHER silently babbles.)* We believed this priest was drinking that altar wine, because you know, they would do this thing of… *(He mirrors the priest in the Catholic ritual of Eucharist, breaking the bread, holding the chalice up, putting it down and solemnly drinking.)* But we always knew that this one had a bit of a, *(FATHER slurps loudly.)* the other priests would come up to the alter, have a taste and the nuns would have their sip, he would have an appreciable *(FATHER gulps.)* So because this particular priest was drunk he'd always twirl as he walked

out. It was always about the arms. We also noticed that
he used to fidget under his robes, playing with something,
presumably his rosary, and we'd watch him waft out
and he would go to the back vestibule, change into a
pair of jean shorts and trainers…into his four by four,
vrrrrroooom, the dust hitting the road. I always wanted to
be like that…a priest I mean.

I got to be class monitor and rather than stop people from
talking I use to incite them. So two things would happen,
the teacher would say, 'OK, you as the class monitor, you
have failed so I'm punishing you' and I'd get a slap. As
the ringleader it made me feel good in front of the guys,
the guys really liked it. Or, we as a collective, as a class,
we would get beaten up, which the studious people in the
group really didn't like, and sometimes they would be like,

STUDENT

I'm sorry, Tonderai was talking.

MAN

As this happened so regularly people just ended up talking
in all of the study times that I was class monitor, because
they thought,

STUDENT

if I don't talk, and the teacher comes, I get slapped
anyways!

MAN

So we would all line up and the teacher would just
smack each person. *(Students line up.)* So you'd have the
anticipation of the moment when you reached there.

STUDENT

(Easing in for the slap.) There was a rumour that went
around that if you were the first one there, then you would
really have an easy time because the teacher would just be
warming up into his strikes.

47

MAN *(Smacking WOMAN as the various students.)*
You'd get a *smack*, then the next person steps up then a *smack*. By the time you have the fifth or sixth person then the teacher is just *(Smack.) (Smack.) (Smack.)*. So you kind of were like,

STUDENT
what do I do to prepare myself, what do I do

MAN
because it's coming to you no matter what happens, it's coming to you. Sometimes the teacher stopped to scratch his hand. Once he was prepped, then another person comes. *(Smack.)* The women teachers were particularly good at it, they would just use their fingers and go *(Smack.) (Smack.) (Smack.) (Smack.)*, and that is way more painful than, you know, going like that *(Smack.)* to you. And then if you were towards the end you'd get a bit of a lighter take on it. But if you were the class monitor you'd definitely get two smacks for that. *(MAN gets two smacks by WOMAN in retaliation.)*

ANOTHER STUDENT
There's a car, there's a car with a woman inside!! She's so glamorous!!!

MAN
So the headmaster called me in and I'm walking toward this blue Mazda 323, I'll never forget it. My dad, my grandmother and my uncle were all there – then my mum just comes out of the car. I must have wept for about forty-five minutes – it's a strange moment you know – 'I don't recognize you but I know it's you.' England had become a dreamland to me. I imagined what it was like, the snow, the tube, the reluctant sun. We drove down to the shops to have our pictures taken. She told my dad that he would bring us to England for a holiday. That was the idea. Mum was very nice to my father, went to his house, met his wife which was very unusual, but when it was time for us to go to England…his air ticket just didn't come.

WOMAN
> That old chestnut aay, where have I heard that before?

MAN
> and, there was the fear that he would cancel everything

MUDHARA
> 'I'll cancel it!' Ndozvikamzura!

MAN
> But, he actually never cancelled anything. Sometimes I wish he had. *(Sound of airplane taking off.)*

CHAPTER 7: ADULTHOOD – UPPER CARE – IDENTITY AWAKENING

At seventeen I progressed to hostel life where you're on your own but staff come and check on you. We got a certain amount of money, you had to budget but they didn't teach you how. I remember one guy bought fifteen loaves of bread 'cause that's what he used to see delivered at the children's home. Money was given on a Friday to last you for the week. I'd be knocking on the door by Wednesday for a sub. I'd also sneak back to the children's home next door for a meal or pick up a bite to take to my room. At the hostel I had a key worker named Joseph who had previously attended the same college as me. His job was to support me in any difficulties I had. We got really close, though we fell out a few times. Mostly because I didn't want to listen to his useful tips.

MAN
> Kemi take advice.

WOMAN
> My mates at college had mentioned to me that he was gay. 'People are saying you are gay Joseph' and he wouldn't say anything. *(JOSEPH says nothing.)* Every now and then I'd say it again. *(Pause.)* *(JOSEPH remains silent.)* I got no response. So I assumed that he wasn't 'gay'. Then one day he said

JOSEPH
'I'm having a birthday party'.

WOMAN
And I said 'I'm gonna come'.

JOSEPH
You can't

WOMAN
So I persisted and he said

JOSEPH
'I asked the head of home if you could come. She said no.'

WOMAN
I got your address and I'm gonna be there anyway.

JOSEPH
Why?

WOMAN
'Cause I wanna come.

JOSEPH
So you mean you'd come despite the authority of the head of home?

WOMAN
Yea.

JOSEPH
Knowing that it could get you in trouble

WOMAN
Yea.

JOSEPH
(Pause.) There's gonna be a lot of gay people there.

WOMAN
(Slight pause.) So.

JOSEPH
And I'm gonna be one of them.

WOMAN

(Pause.) That was my first up close encounter knowing someone who was gay. It was fine with me. I got to go to the party – that's all I cared about. By the time I graduated to bedsit life at eighteen, I was completely on my own.

MAN

No children's home next door for you to sneak back for a meal

WOMAN

No hostel mate down the hall to borrow a quick fiver from

MAN

No one to check up on you.

MAN & WOMAN

It was a cold room

WOMAN

There were no curtains. Just a bare bay window. Boxes with my stuff in it were all around me. I tried to sleep. I couldn't. I went to the off-licence to buy some beer. I never used to drink I didn't like the taste. That night I bought four lagers. I cracked one, then another…then another… and another.

MAN

So you started drinking?

WOMAN

To help me sleep. I was just lonely I guess.

MAN

Really.

WOMAN

(She shrugs.)

MAN

Did the drinking continue? *(She acknowledges the question but doesn't answer. MAN takes note.)*

WOMAN

My first acting job was working with a children's theatre company. That was when I met Christina, the Company Manager. She was tall, funny and smart. I didn't understand why I always wanted to be around her. I found out that she was gay and I thought, hmm, okay that's alright – I like gay people, Joseph, no problem – then I realized that there was something – not that she was just gay but that there was something about me and her – and anyway I went round to her house one day as I had done many times before *(They sit a spell playfully musing. CHRISTINA seems coy about speaking up. WOMAN improvises a few encouraging comments such as 'C'mon', 'what is it'.)* and she said

COMPANY MANAGER

'I'm gay'

WOMAN

She said something about me and her and I flew under the table. I can't remember what she said – but it was something that linked me to her which meant – wait – that's me too – so I sat under the table for a good fifteen minutes. I just couldn't deal with it – I was twenty-one years old. I was okay with everyone else being gay but me… At work sometimes I'd pretend that nothing was happening but it *was (Beat.)* and it *did.*

CHAPTER 8: UK SECONDARY SCHOOL: IDENTITY AWAKENING

LAMAR

You're GAY *(Several students plague him with a barrage of taunts as a discordant version of Choza may be heard in the background.)*

MAN

That's one of the first things I remember hearing on my arrival in England, I soon got used to it. From a mountain outside Harare to Harlesden, North West London, I was not prepared for what was coming to me, as well as the pavement that covered all the soil. I got used to the grey building I was going to spend my time in. This school had no grounds, no swimming pool, no chapel and certainly no priests. There was no sense of control or order. I was attached to another black boy to show me around. Instantly he took a disliking to me, he had already sussed me out and that was the beginning of the nightmare;

NATHANIEL

You're gay man.

MAN

I didn't know what 'gay' meant so I said 'no I'm not' and they kept saying it and I kept denying it. I was confused. I remember this particular boy, his name was Daniel Sennet, he was a bit goofy, buck teeth. He was a really clever bully and he knew how to bring me to my knees with humiliation. Once he made fun of my voice so I wrote him a note saying can you please stop making fun of me…his response?

DANIEL

'He's just written me a love letter!'

MAN

That changed my time at school, everyone believed him. It got to the point where my brother was fighting people and my brother Tanya was like,

TANYA

'Choza, I'm trying my best here but why do you walk like that and why do you talk like that? Why?'

MAN

but I never noticed that I walked differently or talked differently because in Zimbabwe people loved it. I guess my body was changing in ways I did not understand. There was a rumor about me being a girl. I remember looking down just to check. Have you ever done that? Look at your own body in the hope that you see something you had missed all those years? Have you?

MAN

I started becoming what they call androgynous.

WOMAN

The rose was beginning to bloom.

MAN

The toilet at school was a difficult experience. I was always in the corner trying to hide myself. You know the guys, the white guys who really want to intimidate you the second you are at the urinal. *(White STUDENT enters and executes the huge opening of his trouser zipper, as if a small opening would not suffice. He ejects himself while MAN uses another urinal.)* When you're shy and *androgynous* and you're worried about your body then I think you actually become smaller in stature in that situation. Something in me shrunk. You want to just squeeeeeeeze into the corner urinal, hoping no one can see you. And *that's* when they start *talking* to you. They say, while looking at you

STUDENT

'what's up?'

MAN

Then you have to turn. You're worried that if you turn around they will look you up, 'I'm fine.' *(White STUDENT puts himself away then moves to the sink almost imperceptibly trying to catch a peep at MAN as he walks by.)* And they continuously speak to the end.

STUDENT

You see *Match of the Day* yesterday. The ref was blind.

MAN

Even now, I have to take a deep breath before I go into the men's room. When I'm out I make sure that other men on the table have already gone to the bathroom. So there's no…me going to the bathroom and somebody saying 'oh I'll come along with you'. They do that. Men do that ALWAYS. I remember my sports teacher used to say

SPORTS TEACHER

You move like an old woman.

MAN

(Sounds of showers running.) We all had to go into the
showers after PE and he would watch us. *(SPORTS TEACHER
does this.)*

SPORTS TEACHER

You are going to have a shower today.

MAN

And I thought, WELL IT'S NOT YOUR FUCKING
PROBLEM IF I SMELL IS IT? So fucking leave me
alone. But he would stand there and watch us from start to
finish. That adult casting an eye on me, burning into me.

MAN & WOMAN

And me longing to be like everybody else.

MAN

I used to walk home the same route through the park and
one day this guy waves at me. He was in his late twenties I
think, skinny white guy with black hair and he said,

GUY

'You know me'

MAN

And I was like, no I don't, who are you?

GUY

I see you all the time.

MAN

Really, where?

GUY

I see you all time in the park where you play sports.

MAN

'Cause the schools in England don't have grounds so
you have to go to the park for football. In Zimbabwe
everything is in one place. 'Oh you saw me'.

GUY

You were playing football.

MAN

I was always goalie, not a very good one though. Everyone
used to fight to *not* have me in their team. And I thought
that was an interesting thing for him to watch, you know.

GUY

Yeah, anyway I'll see you around. I see you all the time

MAN

And I'm like OK. A day or so later it happens again.

GUY

I saw you walking up the high street. I live quite close to
Harlesden High Street.

MAN

And I thought that's strange, you know, that he'd seen me.
And then the third time

GUY

Yeah I saw you again during sports.

MAN

And then he said,

GUY & MAN

'Do you want to take this path'?

MAN

The park has different paths in it. And I went. And
then my heart started beating faster, you know. 'Cause I
suddenly thought of my brother. I thought, where is Tanya,
where is he? 'Cause I didn't want him to see me walking
with this man. And then he, he, he touched me. This
feeling came over me, the smell of cigarette, the grown up

smell on him. Then he kissed me. And I kind of kissed him back. He asked for my number. I gave it to him. And then he said

GUY

'Don't worry I've got condoms'. *(Pause.)*

MAN

I never saw him again. *That* was my first kiss.

CHAPTER 9: FIRST REAL LOVE > MELTDOWN

WOMAN

Work was good to me in the Eighties. We were on tour in Canada. We got to Winnipeg very late and were told by Tracey, y'know the same 'under the table woman', to go straight to bed because we had an early call in the morning. I did not take her advice. I took myself straight to the bar for a stiff drink.

MAN

Mhmm so it's *stiff* drinks now is it?

WOMAN

That's when I met Tina. She was short, had blond hair with bright blue eyes and a deep voice. Very female. I didn't know what was gonna happen.

TINA

Out of town?

WOMAN

London

TINA

Tequila?

WOMAN

Yes

TINA

Lift?

WOMAN

OK *(They kiss urgently and passionately.)* She said she
had a boyfriend but that didn't stop her from driving
to Edmonton where we booked a hotel during my two
days off and *never* left the room. Thank God for room
service. That was the first time I fell in love, my first real
relationship. When I got back to London we talked on
the phone a lot and I was soo happy. *(The dirge 'Baba ti lo'
emanates from MAN followed by an instrumental version.)*

WOMAN

Then my dad died. I was devastated. The last time I went
to see him in the hospital I felt like I was walking on air. I
knew something was wrong when I approached his room.
The blinds were down and doctors were in front and
behind me. I said 'he's dead isn't he'. I was in such shock.
They asked if I wanted to go in with him but I waited
for one of my aunties to come. All my mates were at the
funeral. After he was buried I felt like I was heading for
chaos. On top of that my sister wanted me to send Dad's
body home to Nigeria. The cost was over two thousand
pounds and there was no way I was going to raise that
money.

MAN

You started drinking heavily didn't you. *(WOMAN is
silent.)* Breathe. We have to tell the truth. *(Pause.)* Those
marvellous African Players who with their backs against
a wall found freedom by telling stories about themselves
instead. You started this. *(He breathes. She breathes.)*

WOMAN

I can't remember a lot of what happened to me when I
drank but the little that was reported to me was frightening

FRIEND

(Exposing her as if already in conversation.) Yes you did!
After we left the pub. We went to this guy's house and got
plastered. You stood in the middle of the sitting room floor,
pulled down your knickers and pissed standing up in front

of everyone. I was so angry I left. But I came back the next day to get you. Sometimes you get downright obnoxious to strangers. Like that time we were walking down the street and you saw this big black woman and went up to her and asked 'Why are you wearing this dress?' And the fight at the club? Surely you remember the fight? *(WOMAN is drunk 'mash up' at the club. Through fault of her own she bumps into a hefty no-nonsense lesbian who attempts to remain calm.)*

WOMAN

Oi watch where you're goin. *(RANDOM GIRL tries to walk away but is further confronted.)* No fuck, no fuck, say sorry… say sorry. *(RANDOM GIRL, still reluctant to get involved attempts to move on.)* You bitch! Bitch.

RANDOM GIRL *(Facing her.)*

What are you doing? What are you doing. *(Unable to resist any longer RANDOM GIRL commences to give WOMAN the beating of her life. After the first blow, wincing in pain…)*

WOMAN:

'You gonna regret that… *(Another blow lands which takes her to the ground. Writhing in pain…)* Now you're really in trouble. *(RANDOM GIRL grabs her by the ear and pulls her to another space as WOMAN screams expletives. She smashes her head atop a bench and woman falls back in total agony. WOMAN crawls behind the bench for refuge and RANDOM GIRL brutally stomps her. There are bloodcurdling screams and then stillness…)*

RANDOM GIRL

You are fucking lucky I decided not to carry my fucking knife today.

WOMAN

I nearly lost my life that night. *(MAN helps her up. He gestures for her to continue her story. She gestures rather – for him to continue. It is a breath moment subtly negotiated between what just happened and what is about to be told.)*

CHAPTER 10: 'DISFIGUREMENT' (TO BE OR NOT TO BE...)

What I *haven't* said is that when I was at school my breasts started growing. I went to the doctor. I was sixteen. At first I thought it was normal 'but after a while' they got bigger and bigger, not really big but 'shapely' as if I was a young girl. I started noticing other things as well, my skin became a different texture. I had only ever seen that type of skin on plums in a fruit bowl. I made my case. *(To the DOCTOR.)* They tease me and say that I'm gay. I get bullied everyday. And now these. I have no confidence, sense of worth or self-respect. I can't swim, shower publicly, take my shirt off, I slouch.

DOCTOR
OK.

MAN
I don't think I'm a girl and I'm worried about what these mean. I want to be normal just like the other kids. I don't want to stand out so much.

DOCTOR
Right.

MAN
As a first step at least I need to get rid of these. I can't go on like this.

DOCTOR
Mmm.

MAN
What was amazing to me was how easy it was to have my doctor refer me to a surgeon who saw the problem and was eager to operate rather than investigate any issues behind a young boy seeking to rid himself of breasts. I guess for him it was routine. I will never know what it meant, what it could mean.

MAN & WOMAN
I remember,

WOMAN
    waking up from surgery

MAN
    bandaged up in what looked like a waiting room

WOMAN
    but was full of people,

MAN
    post-surgery

WOMAN
    with tags on their stretchers

MAN
    waiting to be taken to a recovery ward.

MAN & WOMAN
    I remember

WOMAN
    the confusion

MAN
    that comes from

WOMAN
    waking up from an anesthetic
    and the kind of nightmares you have

MAN
    The constant drowsy feelings you get.

WOMAN
    After being discharged,

MAN & WOMAN
    I remember *(He starts to loosen his top gradually until he is exposed.)*

MAN
    going home with these two vials on either side of my chest

WOMAN
to drain excess blood

MAN
from my scars.

MAN & WOMAN
I remember,

MAN
not having any sensation on my chest,

WOMAN
being bandaged up and waiting

MAN
to have the experience be over so I could

WOMAN
feel

MAN
and become

MAN & WOMAN
normal. *(WOMAN closes his exposed top.)*

MAN
In all those days of recovery, I would have nightmares from the painkillers and wake up relieved and excited that I would have a normal life, just like the other boys. I remember going back to the surgeon a few days later *(SURGEON abruptly examines him.)* and him being excited that the surgery had gone well and that he had managed to do it in a way that meant that I still looked normal. But I didn't feel normal. I just felt disfigured, wrong, one side looked much different to the other, I never really recovered from that. In a way it hardened me. *(SURGEON zips his shirt up.)* After my surgery I went back to school and everything continued just as before except now I felt disfigured, and had to hide the scars too.

WOMAN

The rose had become defiled. *(Pause.) (A breath moment in song. He sings 'Choza'. She joins.)*

MAN

Eventually I convinced myself that I'd gotten used to it and concentrated on school. *(He looks at WOMAN. She continues with her story…)*

CHAPTER 11: HOMELESSNESS

WOMAN

No amount of booze could remove the pain of my dad's death. To make matters worse I became homeless. I ran away for six months to Canada to be with my girl but had made no rent arrangements for my bedsit. When I came back I had to sleep on friends' floors until one night I found myself sleeping underneath a stairwell in Greenwich. *(She shivers curled up.)*

WOMAN

It was dark

MAN

And cold,

MAN & WOMAN

And I was afraid

WOMAN

And every time I heard a voice

MAN

Fear turned to terror,

MAN & WOMAN

Someone could hurt me here.

WOMAN

I felt sick to my stomach. The worst had happened. I was alone. And without a home.

MAN & WOMAN

I realized something had to change. *(A mutual glance.)*

CHAPTER 12. ADULTHOOD: ROCK BOTTOM

Years later as an adult I was still struggling with my body. As far as I was concerned my body was marred. No way was I taking this shirt or trouser off for anyone. The trauma, the bodily changes. I wasn't a guy. Unlike other young men there had been no muscle building, my voice hadn't changed. My shape was somewhat curvy. It was harder for people to tell whether

MAN & WOMAN

I was a boy or girl. *(There is a blatant shift of light. Beat. A visual appears: 'THE AUDITION'. There is a silent re-enactment of the first encounter between MAN & WOMAN. Another image replacing the previous one appears of MAN in his androgynous state. WOMAN looks at him for a long period of time with curious admiration. She seems attracted by something but is not all together certain of what it is.)*

WOMAN

Her smile was beguiling. Like a rose near full bloom. She was different. *(It is a riveting moment between the two, a powerful observation in which MAN is revealed as a woman. A sensuous, alluring, beautiful woman with a subtle air of self-consciousness, a trait which no doubt serves to amplify the attraction. The moment is a slow motion snapshot as natural as first morning's light. WOMAN sits as the image snaps off.)* You're next luv.

MAN

My faith was withering. I went to university to study theology and I came out with a passion for acting. In my mind I became sort of invisible. Even in a gay bar I didn't tick any boxes. I wasn't a 'bear'[4] or a 'cub'[5] or even a 'twink'[6]. I was just indefinable. A grey cloud sunk into

---

[4] Hairy, muscular or stocky, masculine type
[5] Younger version of bear
[6] Usually under 30, without hair, effeminate looking

me. I partied hard. *(Strange music hovers in the air. MAN has been drinking…amongst other things.)* As long as it kept me up I would take it. Misery had found company. I became reckless. Truth is, the more drugs and alcohol I took the harder it was to forget. The thing about coke is that it takes the glint, the sparkle in your eyes away from you and before you know it, you have forgotten how to genuinely smile. I wanted to have sex and walk away. Strangers wouldn't ask questions about my body – I wanted to forget – it didn't matter when, where or how, I just really wanted somebody, I didn't care – if he wanted me, I would be up for it – just the thrill of being touched. Gay, guy sex can be rough and I was ready for anything – it was frightening. It all came to a head one night after a long binge of coke and vodka in Soho. I staggered up to the square park and saw a few men having sex. I managed to sneak in by jumping the fence and walked around the park. I found a guy. *(They start a dance which is at first loose and free, barely touching with the exception of maybe a few turns and the dance becomes more touchy feely in which hands cover bodies off and on in an increasingly passionate way, such that they evolve from caresses to pats, to slaps and invariably sex.)* I didn't care that he wasn't good looking, if he wanted me, I was happy for him to do whatever he wanted me to do. He came to me and started kissing me, the kind of kissing that isn't for pleasure but for dominance – aggressively – as if he was disgusted by the very act of being with me. We started having sex, the kind you have in a park, that is not very comfortable. My phone rang, I recognized the ringtone and reached into my pocket but could not find it, I checked every other pocket and I still could not find it and I finally realized that this guy, who was fucking me, had stolen my phone. I asked for it back and continued to have sex with him. I didn't ask why he had stolen my phone. I didn't care. I just wanted the sex to continue because I felt that's what I needed. Someone having sex with me. From the distance I could hear a police siren approaching and people in the park scattering and jumping the fence to get away. The guy I was with suddenly came on me *(The dance stops.)* and he too scattered, with an agility of someone used to running away from trouble. I was too drunk, too high and at this stage in too much physical pain from sex to actually run away. The police car arrived, lights flashing. It was clear that the policeman was pretending he hadn't seen me to give me time to climb the fence and make a getaway. *(He attempts to jump the fence.)* I couldn't. I was too drunk. I struggled to jump that fence and the policeman averted his gaze once more. I tried again, *(Jumps again.)* I couldn't. I got stuck at the top of the fence. The lights were bright. Spotlighting me. Eventually I fell to the ground and slowly, painfully made my way home. When I woke up the next day

MAN & WOMAN

I realized something had to change.

CHAPTER 13: ONE FOOT FORWARD – FINDING HOME

WOMAN

I've always believed that the ancestors are forever watching over us all

MAN

And firing up others to join the watch, today and in all the tomorrows which fall

WOMAN

From the calm beautiful people whose solitary love ignites our inner glory

MAN

To gentle giants with talking hands who inspire us to tell our stories.

WOMAN

A father

MAN

A brother

WOMAN

    A sister

MAN

    A mother

WOMAN

    A guardian

MAN

    A friend

WOMAN

    A worker

MAN

    A lover *(A drum rhythm occurs or not. If so it is akin to Bata[7] or any African equivalent. It is a rhythm that begins to intensify in consonance with MAN and WOMAN's dance. It is a dance of emerging revelation which simmers at first into a bubble, then bursts into a blossoming rite of passage. MAN and WOMAN invoke the ancestors and the spirits of those present in their lives today who have had an impact on delivering them from a challenging journey. Those who will watch over them tomorrow are also present. Auntie Jane, Tola, Mr Hwamwe, MAMA MAN and many others arrive for the communion. The duo feverishly celebrate them all in dance. The finale is a moment of inspiration in which a cloud lifts. With smiles the celebrants nod nudging MAN and WOMAN forward. A breath moment replete.)*

WOMAN

    I talked to a friend about finding help. She directed me to a Women's Hostel.

HOSTEL WORKER

    Name

WOMAN

    Antonia Kemi Coker

---

[7] A Yoruba ritualistic dance which in secular form enables its followers to sing the praises of those present.

HOSTEL WORKER
Camay

WOMAN
Kemi. K.E.M.I.

HOSTEL WORKER
Age

WOMAN
I'm twenty-six years old.

HOSTEL WORKER
How can I help you?

WOMAN
I've got nowhere to live. Last night I slept on the street.

HOSTEL WORKER
Family?

WOMAN
My mum and dad are dead. I've got an older sister but she's in Nigeria.

HOSTEL WORKER
Friends?

WOMAN
I've got a few friends and have been staying with them on and off.

HOSTEL WORKER
Where were you staying before?

WOMAN
I had a bedsit but I couldn't keep up the rent so I lost it. But I've got a job right now.

HOSTEL WORKER
What kind of work do you do?

WOMAN
I'm an actor. *(HOSTEL WORKER's attention is arrested.)*

HOSTEL WORKER
(Under her breath.) Benefits. *(To WOMAN.)* If everything
checks out we should be able to offer you a place here.
There are a few rules you need to know about.

WOMEN
No problem

HOSTEL WORKER
No drugs

WOMAN
No problem

HOSTEL WORKER
We try to avoid fights.

WOMAN
No problem

HOSTEL WORKER
and no men! *(Beat.)*

WOMAN
No problem.

CHAPTER 14: ONE FOOT FORWARD – TESTOSTERONE

MAN
When I told a friend about what happened in Soho,
particularly about not being safe he suggested that I
seek help. After several tests and examinations another
doctor told me that I was suffering from a condition that
prevented my body from producing testosterone. We
embarked on a series of remedies, most of which did not
work. Finally we resorted to

DOCTOR & MAN
Testosterone Nebido.

DOCTOR

A replacement therapy. Injections once a month.

MAN

Downside?

DOCTOR

The injections are quite painful. Some other side effects include increased weight, mood swings, irritability.

MAN

Upside?

DOCTOR

There are reports of mental agility and hair growth…

MAN

Facial?

DOCTOR

Yes and increased sex drive. There is one other thing you should know.

MAN

Yes.

DOCTOR

If you stop the treatment there will be a reversal of your status. You would probably return to how you are feeling at present.

MAN

I made my decision.

CHAPTER 15: TWO FEET FORWARD – COMING OUT

Coming out. One particular Friday I came home, as I walked in, Mum had been waiting for me, she was sitting at the kitchen table. She was really calm. I was too, although kind of distracted.

MAMA MAN

(Eating groundnuts.) Are you ok?

MAN

> Yes…why?

MAMA MAN

> I don't know, you are not talking. I ask you questions and you don't answer. What's happening?

MAN

> I was going around it but I was *tired* of not saying it, I was *tired* of dismissing THAT as an element, so I was moving into something like: 'but you're my mum and you're my African mum so we're not going to have that conversation' – so she, to her credit, was not giving into that, she was like

MAMA MAN

> So.

MAN

> Then she finally said

MAMA MAN

> 'What is it, are you gay?'

MAN

> and I said 'Yes'. What I really felt like saying was 'I'm sorry'. I wanted to let her know that I didn't want to have failed her in this way. I was really sad. I switched into trying to support her, and to trying to soften the blow – she said

MAMA MAN

> 'Yes I'm fine, I told you I'm fine.'

MAN

> The truth is I could feel her heartbeat from where I was sitting, even though I was positioned opposite her at the kitchen table.

MAMA MAN

> I knew, I just didn't want to say anything. Just in case *you* didn't know. I didn't want to confuse you. *(She offers him some of the groundnuts.)*

CHAPTER 16: THERAPY

MAN

I don't know who it was that suggested…

MAN & WOMAN

That I see a therapist

MAN

But it seemed like a good idea given

MAN & WOMAN

The troubles I'd seen

MAN

The therapist had short dark curly hair. Sort of a bob hairdo

WOMAN

She wore a female trouser suit. Grey.

MAN & WOMAN

They like to look neutral for some reason or the other.

MAN

The first thing I notice when I walk into her office is that she sits me into a chair that has a box of tissues next to it on the side table to my right.

WOMAN

And she sits facing the clock behind me on the wall.

MAN

So right away you understand that these people only have a specific amount of time

WOMAN

Seemed kind of strange to be having my life put on a stop watch.

MAN

And all of them seem to have a repertoire of about five or six questions

WOMAN

> Or statements that they expect you to respond to.

MAN & WOMAN

> How does it make you feel?

WOMAN

> Do you think that perhaps you're over thinking this?

MAN

> What if I say to you that there is no such thing as being normal?

WOMAN

> Everyone is struggling with their own identity. Why is it important for you to define yourself.

MAN & WOMAN

> How are you feeling?

WOMAN

> And they will never answer any of your questions with a satisfactory answer.

MAN

> Always sending the question back to you.

MAN & WOMAN

> 'What do you think?'

WOMAN

> And they try to take notes on the sly – summing you up when you say something of interest to them. For instance, like I would say how I was brought up and she would write

MAN

> 'care'

WOMAN

> And I would mention my partner's name and she would write

MAN

> 'lesbian'

WOMAN

So every time I go there I dress neutral 'cause I don't want her to read anything.

MAN

I always do something that's fun and fabulous before I go to see her. Something that reminds me of me. So when I get there I behave like I'm on TV and I'm being interviewed. And I'm always late, to prompt a question that I know is not in her repertoire so I can mess with her mind before she messes with mine. But she always finds a way to get back on that infernal track.

THERAPIST

Are you always late?

MAN

Only when coming to see you. *(Mischievous smile.)*

THERAPIST

How does that make you feel?

MAN

Normal *(Really feeling on top of the game.)*

THERAPIST

What if I say to you that there is no such thing as being normal.

MAN *(Weakened.)*

And before you know it…

WOMAN

She has you blabbering about all the things that have been affecting you.

MAN

My friend was telling me about his boyfriend who he was having a fight with and they're adopting a kid and I'm really listening, you know, I'm trying to be helpful and these two African men walk in. They walk up and down and then walk outside and then come back and they shout

from the door: 'Are you a boy or are you a girl?' And I was
like seriously, number one you *do not* know me, number
two I'm a stranger in a café, having a coffee with my mate
who's having a *problem*. I don't need to answer *you* about
my gender. They insisted and started describing me; the
way I was sitting, how I was dressed, my scarf, my hair,
my skin. I had to give in and say 'I am whatever you want
me to be.' But they *didn't know* what they wanted me to be
so I decided to tell them I was a guy and they shook their
heads and walked away.

WOMAN

So I'm sitting in this waiting room right? Got to sort out my
housing benefit. There's about fifteen to twenty people in
front of me so I know I'm going to be there for a real long
time. I'm reading my book, chilling, doing my own thing. I
notice people looking at me 'cause what I've got on today
are my jean shorts, trainers and a hoodie. So I'm sitting
down there waiting. This man, he calls out: 'Ms. Coker'. I
get myself up and I walk towards him and this guy walks
straight past me so I'm looking at him, and EVERYONE'S
looking at me, and I'm looking at him and this is the day
when I've been called 'Sonny' one too many times in the
tube. He's looking around for somebody that is ME. So I
turned to the guy I said 'Look, I'm Ms. Coker!! It's me! I'm
Ms. Coker.' And then he goes 'oh yeah yeah yeah yeah
sorry yes I could see that' and he starts flustering through
these papers. I am Ms. Coker! I am a woman alright. You
are shouting out in the middle of – I mean do you know
how bad that is? Everybody's looking, you know I do this
shit for a living. *They pay me*, I can't have people watching
me for no money. I'M MS. COKER ALRIGHT!

THERAPIST

Everyone is struggling with their own identity.
Why is it so important for you to define yourself.

MAN & WOMAN

Because I'm a Woman/Man!

THERAPIST

Hmmmmm. Zhe – *(MAN & WOMAN look at themselves in a quandary.)* zhe, it's a gender neutral descriptive term but also means zivete – live

MAN & WOMAN *(Look at each other once again.)*
What?!?

THERAPIST

It was just a thought out loud on self-definition.

MAN

I don't know about the gender neutral thing…but if zhe means to 'live' call me Zhe anytime. I want to live. And to be free is to live. To be me is to live.

THERAPIST

It wasn't a suggestion. I was just thinking out loud. As you were saying…

MAN

So I'm in a club, *(Rhythm to 'It's Your Birthday' by 50 Cent plays.)* I'm with a bunch of my friends, I've got a broken arm which in the gay world is a very good thing. It makes you look dangerous and fun loving and sporty. Makes you look real good. I see a guy I like, I'm like 'hey, OK'. I'm edging towards him, he's responding, I'm edging towards him, he's responding. And this guy is really polite you know, he's really smiling, 'OK great ya ya ya'. And then he just flips at me 'I seriously don't like girls, I'm sorry, you're not my type.' *(MAN takes over 'It's Your Birthday' song which dovetails into WOMAN's oncoming lines. Music still plays faintly in the background…)*

WOMAN

It's my birthday. I'm out with my friends at a club, got on a long skirt, a lady-like blouse, just cut my hair so I'm looking lady-like fine. We're all chilling out having a good time. After three bottles of wine I need to go to the toilet. This is always stress for me…stress. You know what it's like, there's always a queue. So I'm standing here in the

queue, I've got my skirt on okay, but I can see people
looking at me. I'm getting closer and I'm waiting for
someone to tell me ANY-thing. So I get IN to the toilet
now and the ladies are looking at themselves in the mirror.
I'm not looking at any of them, I'm just trying to focus
and do what I've got to do. Some girl comes up to me and
goes: 'Excuse me' And I say: 'I'm a fucking woman!' And I
lift up my skirt… 'Yeah I know that love but weren't you in
that show *'The Big Life'*. *(Music completely stops.)*

THERAPIST
Do you think that perhaps…you are over thinking this.

WOMAN
(Angrily.) Not really because it has happened so many
times in my life that it is as big as the nose on your face.

THERAPIST
(Taking a note discretely.) 'anger management issues'

WOMAN
I mean wait, you're a therapist right? What if someone
kept calling you a dentist…You wouldn't like that would
you?

THERAPIST *(MAN & WOMAN.)*
What do you think?

MAN
I love having lunch with my mum. My mum is the most
entertaining human being on earth, she talks non-stop.
Talks more than I do about her business, her work, her
grandchildren, how proud she is of me, how I'm this
gorgeous young man on my own journey. And I'm in this
French restaurant with her, we're having a great time and
we're laughing, having champagne, the only time that I've
managed to get her to buy champagne. So this waitress
comes up and goes: 'Ladies, what would you like for
lunch?' My mother who speaks non-stop just stops dead.
She's frozen. Frozen with some sort of embarrassment or
fear or whatever – for five strong minutes – just does not

speak. Finally she goes 'Well obviously you're beautiful darling'.

THERAPIST
How are you feeling?

MAN
Very frustrated, makes you wonder whether it's worth trying to change anything at all.

THERAPIST
(Writes.) 'suicidal tendencies'

MAN
At this point I find good use for the tissues.

WOMAN
She glances at the clock on the sly. I figure I have five minutes left. So I shoot my best shot. I tell her about my BIG mistake.

EPILOGUE

I was helping to audition for a play and this girl came to be seen. She had this interesting smile. There was something about her I just couldn't figure out.

MAN & WOMAN
She was different

WOMAN
Yea. That night I had this strong feeling in my gut that something was wrong. I called up the producer and asked about this person and she said

MAN
'She's a he. Not a she.'

WOMAN
I really felt bad relating to someone as a female when they were actually male. So I got his number and phoned to apologize. I didn't feel like my apology was taken.

MAN

> I hated that audition. Normal auditions have you come in alone, your gender is announced. *(With typical Chuck Mike talkative hands expression.)* This was a group audition – some sort of Chuck Mike invention! On top of it all this woman mistook me for a girl.

WOMAN

> You didn't have a beard then and you had far more weight, kind of shapely.

MAN

> Then she called me to apologize. She told me that it also happens to her

WOMAN

> Yes it does…

MAN

> I had to say wait a minute. 'Cause you have to understand the difference between someone *else* thinking you are a girl and you *living* with a girl inside you. They are two different things. So when I hear that kind of apology it's like pfff!

WOMAN & MAN

> It glanced the ear and bypassed the heart

WOMAN

> His response made me feel like I should do something. So I met up with him and talked to him about creating a play about mistaken gender.

MAN

> Little did we know we'd be doing a play about

MAN & WOMAN

> Our lives

WOMAN

> A story *I* had been putting off for a long time. *(Beat.)* In 1995 I moved from the hostel into permanent housing, I met my current partner and stopped using drink to escape

my problems. I also went to Nigeria to do a play and I saw my sister Tola.

MAN

In 2009, I went back to Zimbabwe as an actor to do a play. I went to see my father. Happy to see me, he'd diminished in stature but had no regrets about how he'd lived his life.

WOMAN

When I saw her we hugged and there were tears. I stayed for a spell with her family. She'd long been married and is the mother of five children and one grandchild.

MAN

After I returned to London I received news that my father had had an epileptic fit, fell into a fire and died. *(Beat.)*

MAN

So I guess really being sorry means never having to say it.

WOMAN

And maybe real forgiveness comes from a special place

MAN & WOMAN

Where people breathe *(They breathe.)* and tell stories about themselves. *(This final breath fills the lungs and enables a telling of stories with a renewed and mounting vigour surpassing anything we've heard thus far.)*

MAN

When I was a child there was a story I heard time and time again. A story about my mother. *(The following lines are delivered by both actors simultaneously, that is, there is a clash of voices while multiple stories update the audience on their lives into present. These stories grow into a cacophony which resounds into the evening air and beyond.)*

WOMAN

Unlike me Tola is small, softly spoken and resilient. She's a school principal and a highly respected leader in her church.

MAN

> As a young girl Mum was terribly burnt by a fire while reading by candlelight. Her arm was gummed to her shoulder and it was believed that she would never use it again.

WOMAN

> It was hard for her to understand that I do believe in God in my own way. She is very caring, loving and protective of me. I never mentioned my sexuality.

MAN

> They didn't think she would marry. So they sent her to school. At best she would have become a nurse or teacher.

WOMAN

> Lagos was beautiful and busy. I found that I was just like those around me.

MAN

> At school she studied hard and exercised her arm until it became fully functional.

WOMAN

> When I came back to London. I walked differently. I was comfortable in my being, in my spirit.

MAN

> She married my father who by all accounts was a highly sought-after catch of the day and became a very successful business woman.

WOMAN

> I now know that I do have family that will look after me. No matter how different we are, we will always be there for each other.

MAN

> My parents had three children, me being the last, the last good thing of a bad situation. I now know that my life, like Mum's is filled with great promise.

WOMAN

I now know, that the little tingling sensation that I feel at the bottom of my feet that works its way up to the top of my head are my ancestors –

MAN & WOMAN

Always carrying me along, always looking over me.
(The clash of voices concludes. Irin Ajo and Garia Nesu swell as the stories of others are on the ready to be told.)

(Visuals appear.)

Since the commencement of the creation of ZHE in late 2009:

Tonderai undergoes monthly testosterone shots.

He has lost a lot of weight and now has facial hair he refuses to shave for fear of it not growing back.

For a period he assumed a gay male identity but now embraces other possibilities.

His mother has returned to Zimbabwe. She still wears Poison.

Antonia has a female partner of almost two decades with whom she is very happy.

After six public sharings of ZHE Antonia finally came out to her sister Tola who said that she loved her no less.

She added that if Antonia were a practising Christian her sexuality would not be as it is.

Testosterone deficiency is increasingly recognised as a significant health problem.

It adversely affects the sexual, physical and psychological health of aging men.

After four years of developing ZHE and at the ripe age of 60 Chuck Mike also sought testosterone therapy.

He still holds group auditions.

SONGS for ZHE

CHOZA

(More of a chant meaning a boy who is a girl)

MUKULUMUKE

Mukulumuke, maa jo f'Olorun mi
Gently, sweetly, I'll dance for my God
O te mi l'orun kin jo f'Olorun mi
It pleases me to dance for my God
Mukulumuke, maa jo f'Olorun mi

IRIN AJO

Irin ajo l'a wa yi o
We're on a long-distance journey
Ori gbe wa dele o
May our spirit guides/heads deliver us home

Baba ti lo
Baba ti lo
Father has gone
A o ri Baba mo o
We don't see Father anymore
Sun re, Baba
Sleep well, Father

GARAI NESU

Garai nesu mambo wedu, onai tiri vana venyu
Lord be with us, we are your children,
Tinokumbira kunemi, tipeyi tsitsi dzenyu zhingi.
We look to you Lord, to grant us your mercy

ZHE DEVELOPMENT CHRONOLOGY

The ZHE creational trail activity was interspersed with space for meditation and reflection. The following are significant highlights which occurred towards bringing the production into being:

July 2009 – London UK, Oval House Theatre
- Chuck does interviews separately with Antonia and Tonderai uncovering essential memories from childhood to adulthood.
- Soho Theatre is deemed the space for ZHE to run in London and positive discussions are held with the Artistic Director, Lisa Goldman.
- Collective Artistes seek funding for further development of the play and to produce it.
- Transcriptions commence.

January – May 2010 – Virtual Space between the US and UK

- Company members confer via Skype intermittently.
- Chuck does not allow Tonderai and Antonia to be aware of each other's stories yet.

August 2010 – London UK, Hackney Empire
- In a one day workshop improvised 'slams' are created. They explore situations of mistaken identity which have occurred in the lives of Antonia and Tonderai. This later becomes the core of the 'Therapy' scene. Some theatre games are played. More improvisation around 'key words' from the interviews is prompted.

January 2011 – The University of Richmond, Richmond, Virginia USA

- Chuck facilitates a new space away from their usual habitat for the company to reflect more deeply on the work. For two weeks the company is hosted by Chuck and his wife in a serene and white post-Christmas atmosphere.
- The first 'outsider' (Cheyenne Varner, a university student) that would be privy to details of Antonia and Tonderai's lives is brought in to assist.
- Transcriptions are reviewed with the actors separately. Childhood memories are a major focus.
- Chuck uses non-verbal methodology to finally get Antonia to confront the moment she was sexually abused as a child. This leads to more exploration through improvisation and physicalisation of selected interview moments for both actors.

- Antonia and Tonderai are finally privy to the entire contents of each other's stories. The revelation is cathartic for the company.
- Selected bits are rehearsed and shared with an enthusiastic and discerning university audience.
- In the post-show discussion Antonia notes that she cannot come out to her sister but does not mind if Tola encounters the play.

July 2011 – Harare, Zimbabwe
- On a two week expedition the company is received in Harare by a central character in the play; Tonderai's mum. She is more impactful than the pictures painted of her.
- The trio retreat further to the Eastern Highlands (mountains) to a secluded cabin. Members cook and clean for each other and exchange personal stories around a beaming fireplace into the night. Bonding is fortified.
- Fire as a thematic emblem emerges when Tonderai exposes that his father died in a fire and his mother was severely burned in her youth.
- Chuck allocates certain sections of the writing for the actors to complete.
- The company conducts a Forum Theatre workshop at Tonderai's old boarding school where they meet another seminal character; Mr. Hwamwe, Tonderai's old teacher. He is the only teacher from Tonderai's past who still remains at the school.
- A reading of selected material is 'covertly' done in Harare for an audience of Zimbabweans largely of the LGBTQ community. It is a tense period for the company given the draconian laws of the Zimbawean government against gay rights. The trio meet some of those who have been persecuted. Audience members clamour for more information to be placed in the text regarding the treatment of gay people in Africa.

August 2011 – London, UK, Soho Theatre
- Lengthier portions of the would-be draft of *ZHE* is read before a responsive audience of theatre colleagues, friends and LGBTQ community members. In the bar the textual notions get first-hand UK critical appraisal.
- Lisa Goldman has left Soho as its Artistic Director. The Associate Director and dramaturge Nina Steiger offers copious notes for further development.

January 2012 – A Stranded Hotel in Richmond Virginia

- Chuck goes to the 'mattress'. Hiding out in a bleak and bare hotel room for about a week he attempts to bring cohesion to the play structure before its first preview staging next month.
- The various dramaturgical responses to the work so far are also under consideration including the need for a voice on the African condition regarding gay rights.
- Chuck resolves to address several challenges, most significantly; 'why are these two stories being told together'. A prologue and epilogue are created as a structural format.
- Antonia has retreated on holiday somewhere unknown and Tonderai is in Germany working. Finally after a lengthy period of soul searching and wrestling with the ideas of the story Chuck gets hold of Tonderai via Skype. The two have mutually inspiring and supportive conversations. During this period Tonderai alludes to his growth in the context of androgyny and for the first time refers to it in terms of beauty. The metaphor of 'the rose' emerges.

February 2012 – London, UK, Canada Water Culture Space, Tara Arts Centre, New Wolsey Theatre and Leeds University Workshop Theatre

- Prior to upcoming rehearsals Tonderai is more candid about his search for help against the landscape of a sexual escapade in Soho park under the influence of drugs. He also speaks about his painful feelings around growing breasts as a young boy.
- ZHE begins its 'preview tour' starting at Canada Water Culture Space which is located in a library. Having worked in tranquil and protective conditions the company is thrust into its first mainstream theatre environment with all of the attendant bureaucratic mores.
- Antonia makes known her deepest fears about discussing the period of her life around alcohol abuse.
- There is great 'opening' performance tension. Chuck is ready to yank the show if the pressure to perform appears to be detrimental to the health of the actors and makes them aware of this.
- For the first time youth are brought to see the material and interact with the performers.
- A part-time producer from Soho Theatre attends and demonstrates 'interest'.
- At Tara Arts the inclusion of a clash of voices towards the end of the play is introduced, the actors will end their stories speaking simultaneously.
- Gay youth present speak out and thank the company for voicing 'their' stories as well.
- After Leeds and New Wolsey the set undergoes a strip down to bare basics. An intended rap, music and dance which speak to

African gay oppression is cut for lack of understanding how best to implement it with artistic truth.

- The question arises as to 'who are the characters talking to in the play, who are they answering?' Chuck is convinced by the duo that his role in the play must be given visibility and sections of the script making reference to him are incorporated.
- After the performances Antonia reasons that being honest about herself is tantamount to ZHE's credibility as part of the machinery for making change in the world. She comes out to her sister.

July 2012 – London, African Centre
- A one week workshop and showcase sharing at The African Centre serves as a warm-up for the US preview tour. The event also hopes to get more UK venues interested in the show – especially Soho Theatre. (The producer who saw it at Canada Water has left Soho Theatre.)
- For the first time the company gives more detailed attention to the play outside of their roles as creators. In rehearsals more study is given to the perspectives of the characters and the relationships between each other.
- Someone very close to Chuck and whom he has known for several decades decides to come out to him. Chuck hadn't a clue.

August – September 2012
- Discussions intensify with Soho Theatre's new Artistic Director, Steve Marmion for ZHE to be presented there.
- The character names in the script change from Antonia and Tonderai to MAN and WOMAN to give the script more universality.

January 2013 – Richmond and Louisiana, USA
- The company lands at the Firehouse Theatre in Richmond in the middle of controversy. There are picket lines outside the theatre. The demonstration has nothing to do with ZHE but according to them, is a reaction to the unjust firing of the Firehouse Artistic Director by the theatre's board. The protesters organise an additional performance of ZHE for themselves at the legendary Hippodrome Theatre. The play becomes a tool for mitigating conversations around the local strife.
- ZHE returns to the University of Richmond, Modlin Center and proceeds to Centenary College in Louisiana where it is the centrepiece for the Martin Luther King Jr. annual celebration.
- Physical (touching) interaction between adults and youth in the public school system in America is taboo. After a workshop at a nearby secondary school in Louisiana one young student asks a final question: Can they hug the company members?
- The US preview revisions include implementing a projected prologue and epilogue. The first encounter between Antonia

and Tonderai is also recalled and heightened in the middle of the play by lighting and photographic effects. Additionally the stateside tour simplified the paint designs in the set. Having played in most intimate spaces of 150 or less, in Centenary *ZHE* was shown in a venue which sat over 300 people. The actors had filled the space with their personas. Most performances in the US received standing ovations.

February 2013 – Hertfordshire and Folkstone UK

- The preview tour had its final performances in the UK at The University of Hertsfordshire and the Quarterhouse Theatre in Folkstone. While the latter showing wound up the tour with resounding aplomb the university workshop was specifically commissioned for doctoral clinical psychologists in training. The clinical lecturer in charge (Dr. Lizette Nolte) notes in her correspondence to colleagues in her field at various other universities she would like to take on the play; 'The play addresses many aspects relevant to clinical psychology, including the intersection of culture, migration, gender and sexuality; the ways stories are told and heard; how our own views, perceptions and experiences influence what we can hear and see; the importance of human connection first and foremost; and so much more. However, what made the day the significant training experience that it was, was mostly the two actors themselves, who created a context where emotional and relational risk-taking and "being seen" allowed for rich personal connection and reflection and the creation of a deeply moving training experience.' Her students write positively about the performance and its impact on them as people and budding therapy practitioners.
- For several months Chuck has complained of listlessness and excessive tiredness. Though doctors diagnose exhaustion Chuck insists on having his testosterone level checked. It is discovered to be far below normal.

July 2013 – London, Soho Theatre

- A final two week workshop is done taking into consideration the preview tour changes. For the first time the company 'rehearses' the play. Antonia and Tonderai give full attention to 'acting'. Chuck also focuses on 'directing' the play microscopically. They explore with intense depth the moments and beats of the play. The extent of Antonia's drunkenness is made more explicit by a choreographed fight in which she is nearly beaten to death. These rehearsals result in a more complex, vivid, clearer, occasionally light-hearted and more celebratory effect. A sharing before Soho Theatre staff and an audience of over 40 people is met with several standing ovations.
- Tickets for Soho Theatre London performances of *ZHE* in November 2013 go on sale a week after the sharing.

'WHY'

Seiki Pe Kini
Why do I have to be tormented every day
because I look one way
and am another
Why do I yearn to be a man
When there's a woman inside me making demands
Why can't people see the beauty in me
Seiko Pe Kini
Why can't the world just let me be.
Why am I making apologies
Because I insist on being free
Free Free Being Free Free Free Being Free
Why do I live in an oppressive state
Protecting our families against the hate
Mother Father, Sister Brother
Cousins, Aunties, all the others
There is no way that I can guarantee
That the hatred will only be directed at me
In Africa the clan has rules and
Government laws created by fools
MALAWE, KENYA, ZIM, NIGERIA
Infested with homophobic hysteria
Why Why Why Why Why Why Why Why
Why do I live under threat every day
Any time my life could be taken away
Why must I walk with blood on my back
When they beat me, laugh and have a good chat
Why am I sentenced to 14 years

With a crowd watching on waiting to cheer

Why am I hung or burned alive

WITH MY LAST BREATH HEAR MY CRY

Whyyyyyyyyyyyyyyyyyyyyyyyyyyyyyyyyyyyyyyyyyy

Seiko Pe Kini

The potential for greatness

Lies in both genders

Why can't we

BENDER THIS GENDER

'WHY' was initially used during the therapy scene by MAN and WOMAN with original music and choreography. We have placed it in the publication particularly for those in Africa whose voices clamour to be heard on gay rights.

PRODUCTION NOTES

The Collective Artistes production SETTING for *ZHE* used four benches and a platform all shaded white and splattered with black spots. An accompanying floor design in the same colours was also used diagonally protruding from the base platform veering largely towards Stage Right. All set pieces worked best when placed in an all black space. The COSTUMES consisted of two black custom made differently cut trousers with matching hoodies; two pairs of sneakers, one pink and white (WOMAN), the other orange and white (MAN). Two scarves were also part of their adornment; one pink and the other orange. The scarves were also used for character changes as well as props such as pool sticks and a microphone amongst many others.

Most showings of *ZHE* concluded with a post performance talk back and in many of these instances professionals savvy on LG-BTQ affairs were in attendance to handle audience questions and to support those who may have been affected by the performance.

IF YOU HAVE BEEN AFFECTED BY ANY OF THE ISSUES IN ZHE AND WANT TO DISCUSS THEM, PLEASE CONTACT:

UK:

TERRENCE HIGGINS TRUST: (www.tht.org.uk/) Tel. 0808 802 1221

STONEWALL: (https://www.stonewall.org.uk/)Tel 0808 502020

GENDERED INTELLIGENCE: (http://www.genderedintelli-gence.co.uk) Tel. 07841291277 for trans youth and gender identity; 07950471414
for trans awareness training and 07540 261104 for general enquiries.

US:

GLBT NATIONAL HELP CENTER: (http://www.glnh.org/) 1800 843 4564

CREDITS

ANTONIA KEMI COKER (Co-Author/Woman) is a performer with over 25 years experience working nationally and internationally in regional and West End theatre, TV and Radio as well as the fields of Young People's theatre, Forum Theatre, Street Theatre, site-specific, and on-site role play. As well as performing in Collective Artistes' *Things Fall Apart, Yerma, Ikpiko: Sense of Belonging* and *The African Company Presents Richard III*, Antonia has played lead roles in *The Big Life* (Apollo/Theatre Royal), *African Snow* (York Theatre Royal), *Ragamuffin* (UK Tour) and *Lear's Daughters* (Yellow Earth) and a Guardian in *Babel*. For many of her performances, she draws on her strong singing voice and skills in African dance and percussion. Her performances are consistently noted by critics as 'powerful' and some of the strongest amongst her peers. Her training in theatre has mainly come through devised projects.

TONDERAI MUNYEVU (Co-Author/Man) Credits include Othello in *Othello* (Rose Theatre, Kingston and the Watermill Theatre), Proteus in *The Two Gentlemen of Verona* (Two Gents/Shakespeare's Globe), the Lead Man in *ZHE* (UK Tour), Hearts Unspoken (Tron Theatre Glasgow), *Harare Files* (International Tour), *Yours Abundantly*, From Zimbabwe (Oval House) and *The Merchant of Venice* (Arcola). He is a founding member of Two Gents Productions whose international tours have included *Hamlet, Two Gentlemen of Verona* and *Magesti*. His film debut was in *The Day of the Triffids* (HBO/BBC Films) and he has just shot the role of Peter in the feature *Something Nice from London*.

CHUCK MIKE (Co-Author/Artistic Director) is an award-winning, internationally acclaimed theatre maker, director, producer and social activist. Some of his main-stage productions have appeared on the stages of the Kennedy Center in Washington D.C., the Royal Court Theatre in London, the Edinburgh Festival and the National Theatre in Lagos, Nigeria. Some highlights include: *Fences, Raisin in the Sun, Macbutu* (after *Macbeth*), *Death and the Maiden, The Crucible, Things Fall Apart, Yerma, Women of Owu* (after *Trojan Woman*), *Tegonni* (after *Antigone*), *The African Company Presents Richard III* and *The Meeting*. His passion is initiating devised performances for social change and he has done so in rural and urban communities across Africa, Europe and North America. Seminal to these efforts and developed for the formal stages of the UK is *Sense of Belonging* (The Tale of Ikpiko), a play on female circumcision in Nigeria. He has been artiste-in-residence/workshop leader and educator in leading academic and artistic institutions globally. Among these include University of Leeds, Oxford University, University of Toronto, New York University, University of Ife, Nigeria, London's Royal National Theatre Studio and the Windybrow Center of Johannesburg, South Africa. Highlighting his producing efforts has been four festivals/seasons of theatre for CAFTAN (Collective Artistes Festival of Theatre Arts Nigeria). Founding Artistic Director for Collective Artistes (Nigeria and UK) and The Performance Studio Workshop of Nigeria, Chuck Mike has been the recipient of awards from Fulbright/International Telephone and Telegraph, MacArthur Foundation, Ford Foundation and the American Cultural Specialist program. Also an Associate Professor of Theatre at the University of Richmond, Richmond, Virginia, USA he is married with three lovely 'productions'.

JUWON OGUNGBE (Musical Composer) is an inspiring and well-respected musician, singer, composer and band leader from London, of Nigerian heritage. Placing African music at the heart of his work, Juwon also incorporates pop, jazz and classical music into his expressive range. Juwon's concert and music theatre compositions consistently attract interest from theatre and dance practitioners. Commissions include music for the Royal Shakespeare Company, Union Dance and the Southbank Centre amongst many others. *Life Force Music* – Juwon's debut album, released to wide acclaim in 2012 is available via his site www.juwonogungbe.com, at http://juwonogungbe.zimbalam. com and at live events.

KATE UNWIN (Designer) has worked as a freelance set and costume designer for twelve years. Highlights include *The West End Men* (Milton Morrissey Ltd) Vaudeville Theatre, *Vanessa and Virginia* (Moving Stories) at Riverside Studios (nominated for Best Set Design in the Off West End Awards), *Ready Steady Cook* (Stage Version), *Melody Loses Her Mojo* (20 Stories HIgh) Liverpool Everyman, *Cymbeline* (Phizzical Productions) Coventry Belgrade and touring, *Refugees of the Septic Heart* (Tom Dale Company), *FIB* and *Trackdown* for Metro-Boulot-Dodo (National Theatre), *The Beginning* (Michael Pinchbeck), *Girls Night No. 1 Tour* (Goodnights Entertainment), *A Christmas Carol* in Wormwood Scrubs Prison (Only Connect), *The Book Of Everything*

(National Theatre Connections), *ZHE: [noun] undefined* and *The African Company Presents Richard III* (Collective Artistes), *Godspell* number one tour (Oftrot Productions), *Animal Farm* (Derby Playhouse), *Hot Stuff, To Kill a Mockingbird, An Ideal Husband, Macbeth, The Cripple of Inishmaan,* all for Leicester Haymarket Theatre where Kate worked extensively designing for the main stage, studio and foyer spaces. Site-specific and installation work includes *C-Attack* in Great Yarmouth (Dende Collective), Special Olympic Village, Street Style Sport Style exhibition, transformed shopping unit for Leicester Highcross opening weekend and a solo project celebrating the life of Joe Orton. Art Direction for music video includes work for Example, Scouting For Girls, Iglu and Hartley, Leo Ihenacho and Lil' Chris. Set and costume design for many commercial clients including Lynx, Pepsi, Doritosand, an award-winning advert for Samsung.
www.kateunwin.co.uk

CIS O'BOYLE (Lighting Designer) is a London-based lighting designer & performance maker. Choosing to work collaboratively the breadth of her practice has included large-scale installations, architecture, exhibitions, film, theatre and narrative environments. Recent work has been seen at the ICA, Barbican, Sydney Opera House, Natural History Museum, The Place & The Roundhouse. With her collaborators she has been awarded the Oxford Samuel Beckett Award and two Fringe First Awards. She is a guest lecturer for several London universities and has published lighting research for the Institute of Lighting Professionals & the Institute for Live Arts Research.

W. REED WEST III (Projection Designer) has been creating light and scenic design for more than thirty years. He has been the resident designer at the University of Richmond in Virginia for nearly three decades. After receiving his BA in speech and theatre at the University of Richmond, Mr. West completed his MFA in Design and Technical Theatre at Wayne State University. He has created scenic and lighting designs for the University of New Orleans, St. Mary's College of Maryland, The Civic Theatre of Central Florida, The Hillberry Repertory Theatre and SUNY Plattsburg. While on sabbatical in 1992, he was the technical assistant at the Royal National Theatre in London, England. In the fall of 1999, Mr. West returned to England at Stratford-Upon-Avon where he worked with the Royal Shakespeare Company, and in 2008 worked with the Abbey Theatre in Dublin. In addition to his design duties at the University of Richmond, he has also designed for Samara Drama Theatre (The Max Gorky Theatre) in Samara, Russia; St. Joseph's University in Philadelphia and has two productions at the Theatre for Youth in Saratov, Russia. Most recently, he designed *Barefoot In the Park* for the Russian Drama Theatre in Ufa, Republic of Bashkortostan

ANDILE SOTIYA (Choreography) is a South African-born dancer, teacher, choreographer who has worked in the industry for well over a decade. A former Associate Artist at The Place he has danced with Phoenix Dance Company/Theatre and Ludus Dance Company. He has also toured with Kylie Minogue's Fever World Tour and Showgirl Home Coming Tour working with choreographers Rafael Bonachela, Akram Khan and Michael Rooney. Additional work with Kylie incudes; MTV European Awards in Edinburgh, *Top of the Pops*, *CDUK* and a tour of America. Founder of **dancenomad**, his research, choreographic, consultation and production outlet, *STADIUM* (2003) his first full evening creation was performed at the Robin Howard Dance Theatre, The Place in London and at The Riley Theatre in Leeds. Subsequent performances were in South Africa and at the Harare International Festival of Arts (HIFA) in Zimbabwe. He has choreographed for Phoenix Dance Company, Union Dance Company, Mozambique National Dance Company of Music and Dance, and Ace Dance and Music. His Youth work incudes; National Youth Dance Company, Northern Youth Dance Company, Hampshire Youth Dance Company, Advance Youth Dance Company in Leeds, Swindon Youth Dance Company and a residency in Belfast working with young artist from the two communities. He has also created works for Northern School of Contemporary Dance, London Contemporary Dance School and Tshwane University of Technology (former Technikon Pretoria) and Ikapa Dance Theatre both in South Africa. Andile is a founder member and co-director of RODA, a collective that facilitates a very successful Leeds-based research and development residency. With the Fifa World Cup hosted by South Africa in 2010, Andile worked with South African Tourism in promoting the games and the spirit of South Africa, producing events in Davos, Switzerland, Wembley Stadium, Emirates Stadium, Manchester Conference Centre, Olympia Exhibition Centre to name but few. His other credits include movement direction for *Who Killed Mr Drum* for Treatment Theatre directed by Paul Robinson (Riverside Studios, London). Movie credits include *Hunky Dory* directed by Marc Evans featuring Minnie Driver. Andile started his relationship with Collective Artistes and director Chuck Mike on the first preview outings of

ZHE:[noun] undefined in January 2012. Recently he also worked on the development of *Threshold* (Pleasance Theatre, London, July 2013). As a teacher he has taught extensively around the UK and in South Africa leading classes, workshops and residencies from beginners to professionals. He has also taught company classes for DV8, *Lion King,* to name but a few. Andile is also involved in the training of the Billy Elliot company (*Billy Elliot the Musical*) including workshops, auditions and summer intensives. He is currently a Lecturer at the Northern School of Contemporary Dance in Leeds.

ROBIN COLYER (Fight Director) is a qualified stage combat teacher under the British Academy of Dramatic Combat (BADC) and the Academy of Performance Combat (APC). Robin has taught for a number of leading drama schools, including Guildford School of Acting, Royal Welsh College of Music and Drama, Oxford School of Drama and East 15. In addition to his work as an independent fight director, Robin is an Artist in Residence at Oxford Playhouse in his role as artistic director for emerging theatre company, Flintlock Theatre.

NATALIE DAVIS (Technical Stage Manager) is a graduate of Trinity College Carmarthen Wales. She holds a BA in Theatre Design and Production. Her work in Touring Theatre has been vast and she has served as Technical Manager and Lighting Designer for various theatre companies around the UK. With The Young Shakespeare Company and School History Scene her work includes *Macbeth*, *Romeo and Juliet*, *The Tempest* and several British Historical Plays. Significant to her many event tours is a stint with 80s pop star David Essex. In her varied career positions in Management and Design Natalie has also worked at the Pleasance Theatre, London on its comedy revues. In the US Natalie has worked for Stage Door Manor Performing Arts Centre where she now serves as Head Lighting Designer and Electrics (LX) Team Leader. Her productions with them include *Les Misérables*, *Young Frankenstein*, *Chicago*, *Phantom of the Opera*, *The Wiz* and *High School Musical*. Natalie is excited about her work in the US and looks forward to her continued residency there.

OLUSOLA OYELEYE (Producer) is an award-winning writer, director and producer working in opera, music theatre, visual arts and dance. She studied physical theatre at L'École Internationale de Théâtre Jacques Lecoq in Paris, writing at the National Film and Televison School, Beaconsfield and has an MA in Contemporary Theatre Practice and Psychology from the University of Essex. Olusola is also an experienced dramaturge. As Producer for Collective Artistes: *Threshold* by Oladipo Agboluaje (2014/15 international tour); *ZHE: [noun] undefined* (Soho Theatre/UK tour); (associate producer), *The African Company Presents Richard III*. As Director includes: *A Wing, A Pray, A Song* (Guest Projects Africa, Yinka Shonibare Studio); *Heartbeat, the Musical* (Garden Theatre); *Tin* (The Lowry), *Scenes from Ti-Jean and his Brothers* (Collective Artistes & Sustained Theatre, National Theatre, Cottesloe; Resident director on Trevor Nunn's West End production of *Porgy and Bess* (Savoy Theatre); staff producer at English National Opera; *Spirit of Okin and Sankofa* for Adzido Pan African Dance Ensemble, (National & International tours), the award-winning *Call Mr Robeson* (UK tours, New York Fringe & Carnegie Hall; *Coming Up For Air* (The Drum & UK tour); *The Resurrection of Roscoe Powell* (Soho Theatre); *The Shelter* (Royal Shakespeare Company, Barbican Theatre; *Medea* (Ariya, Royal National Theatre Studio); *The Playground* (Polka Theatre, Time Out Critics' Choice Pick of the Year); *High Life* (Hampstead Theatre); *Maybe Father*, (Talawa, Young Vic), *Twelfth Night* (British Council Tour, Zimbabwe) and *Ella*, a monodrama about Ella Fitzgerald (Rich Mix). Opera includes: Akin Euba's, *Orunmila's Voices: Songs from the Beginning of Time* (Jefferson's Arts Centre, New Orleans) and *Chaka: An Opera in Two Chants* with the St. Louis African Chorus, *Dido and Aeneas* (Tricycle/BAC), *God's Trombones* (Fairfield Halls) and the second cast revival of Jonathan Miller's production of *The Mikado* (English National Opera). Olusola has also worked in Ghana, South Africa, Zimbabwe, Nigeria, Hungary and the Czech Republic. She has been a visiting lecturer and Artist at Witswatersrand University, Johannesburg and the Centre for Continuing Education (CENCE) at University of Port Elizabeth, South Africa; also Goldsmith's and Middlesex Universities, London, and she was Head of the Acting Studio at Morley College. Her poetry has been set to music by Akin Euba and performed at both Harvard and Cambridge Universities. Olusola is artistic director of Ariya, producer for Collective Artistes, and the UK co-ordinator for the symposium: Composition in Africa and the Diaspora, held bi-annually at Cambridge University. She is a Fellow of the Royal Society for the Arts.

www.ingramcontent.com/pod-product-compliance
Ingram Content Group UK Ltd.
Pitfield, Milton Keynes, MK11 3LW, UK
UKHW031250020325
455689UK00008B/125